KEEPING

LENT

&

EASTER

KEEPING LENT & EASTER

DISCOVERING *the* RHYTHMS *and* RICHES *of the* CHRISTIAN SEASONS

LEIGH HATTS

DARTON · LONGMAN + TODD

First published in 2017 by
Darton, Longman and Todd Ltd
1 Spencer Court
140–142 Wandsworth High Street
London SW18 4JJ

ISBN 978-0-232-53337-8

A catalogue record for this book is available from the British Library.

Designed and produced by Judy Linard

Printed and bound in Great Britain by Bell & Bain, Glasgow.

CONTENTS

INTRODUCTION

D. H. Lawrence recognised 'the inward rhythm of man and women' when he wrote of 'the sadness of Lent, the delight of Easter, the wonder of Pentecost, the fires of St John, the candles on the graves of All Souls', the lit-up tree of Christmas, all representing kindled rhythmic emotions in the souls of men and women...'.

Pastor Iuventus, author of *Diary of a City Priest*, recently reflected on the dangers of moving the observance of special days: 'Everything about human anthropology would tell us that the body and mind are attuned to the subtlest rhythms. In dividing our calendar with God's time we were acknowledging that such rhythms are part of our God-created, redeemed humanity.'

'Seasonality teaches us patience and restraint,' says chef Claire Ptak who sells hot cross buns only on a few days prior to Good Friday at her Violet Bakery in London's Dalston.

Keeping Lent and Easter continues the journey followed in *Keeping Advent and Christmas* by picking up the liturgical year at Shrovetide.

So after enjoying pancakes, or even an ancient Shrove football game, we can undertake a long journey through Lent and go up to Jerusalem with Jesus for Passover. Easter only makes sense if you have lived out the forty days of Lent and its Holy Week climax. 'There can be no carnival without the ensuing Lent and without these rhythms life is a featureless flatland,' claimed Richard Chartres when he was Bishop of London.

Blessed John Henry Newman, preaching at St Mary the Virgin Oxford in 1838, said: 'None rejoice at Eastertide less than those who have not grieved in Lent. This is what is seen in the world at large. To them one season is the same as any other, and they take no account of any. Feast day and fast day, holy tide and other tide, are one and the same to them. Hence they do not realise the next world at all.' Lent is an opportunity to renew our friendship with God.

'What we celebrate is ancient and stands for deep continuities and rituals without which people become disorientated,' said Bishop Chartres when taking part in Beating the Bounds of his home parish on the eve of Ascension Day.

The liturgy in church is the apex of the church's life and anyone can participate at the parish church as much as in Jerusalem and Rome. There can also be much pleasure in rediscovering the seasonal Christian-based customs buried deep within culture and liturgy.

Leigh Hatts

Date of Easter

The date of Easter determines when Lent begins. The Council of Nicaea, which gives the earliest mention of Lent, agreed in 325 that Easter Day should be the first Sunday after the full moon on or after 21 March. However, for simplicity the equinox is taken as falling on 21 March so Easter does not always correspond to the date of the Jewish Passover. Easter Day can be between 22 March and 25 April. Shrove Tuesday, coming forty-one days before Easter, could fall on 3 February which is the day after Candlemas. This last occurred in 1818 but will not happen again until 2285. The next time Easter Day falls on the latest possible date is 2038.

The Orthodox Church keeps the old calendar which means that Easter Day can be in early May and only occasionally coincides with the Western date.

BEFORE LENT

Sunday Before Lent
Quinquagesima
Transfiguration Sunday

Today, or very early in Lent, the Church recalls the Transfiguration of Christ which marked the moment his teaching ministry gave way to the start of the long journey to Jerusalem. It was also an anticipation of Easter. The Transfiguration not only confirmed Christ's role but today can inspire a transfiguration, or marked change, of life by the coming Lenten observance.

In the Lutheran Church, today is known as Transfiguration Sunday. Quinquagesima Sunday, an ancient name first used in the sixth century, comes from this being the fiftieth day before Easter including Sundays. The forty days of Lent are sometimes referred to as Quadragesima.

The Transfiguration
Matthew 17.1-9, Mark 9.2-10 and Luke 9.28-36
The Transfiguration appears in the calendar on 6 August although the event probably occurred in November around five months before Christ's death on the cross. The August date was chosen in 1457 in thanksgiving for the Christian victory against the Turks at the siege of Belgrade on 6 August 1456.

Six days after Jesus first made it clear to his disciples that he was going to Jerusalem, where he would suffer, he took Peter, James the Great and John up Mount Tabor to witness his Transfiguration. Christ appeared in a shining light with Moses and Elijah, as a voice spoke of Jesus as 'My son, my chosen'. This was the ratification of Jesus' divine nature and an assurance for him as he is shown as the successor to Moses and Elijah representing both the Law and the Prophets and change.

According to the Roman Catholic Ceremonial of Bishops, 'The annual observance of Lent is the special season for the ascent to the holy mountain of Easter'. The Orthodox Church believes that the Transfiguration is the first time in Christ's life that the glory of God is visible. The second occasion is the resurrection (see page 100).

On Maundy Thursday (see page 71), the same three Apostles were close to Christ in the Garden of Gethsemane as he was arrested. In 2011 Benedict XVI said that it was by means of the Transfiguration that 'the Disciples were prepared for the Paschal mystery of Jesus: to overcome the terrible trial of the Passion and to better understand the luminous truth of the resurrection'.

In Church

In the Anglican Church the gospel is the story of the Transfiguration. It is read in the Roman Catholic Church on the Second Sunday of Lent. Today is the last Sunday until Easter Day when the Alleluia will be heard before the gospel reading. It is also the last Sunday where there are flowers in church (except sometimes on Mothering Sunday). Palm crosses from last year should be brought back to church today to be made into ashes (see page 34).

Tis good, Lord, to be here! is a Transfiguration theme hymn.

Shrove Tuesday

Today is the last day before the start of Lent and is known in England as Shrove Tuesday or Pancake Day. *Shrove* is derived from *shrive*, meaning to *confess* sins. Making pancakes used up all the fat in the household before Lent when there would be fasting and plain food. The earliest pancake recipe is 1430. Shakespeare includes the line 'a pancake for Shrove Tuesday' in *All's Well That Ends Well* written in 1604.

Some people not only eat pancakes before Lent but also avail themselves of the sacrament of reconciliation (confession) (see page 62).

Once the last day before the great fast was kept with much more exuberance, but the Reformation began the gradual decline in today's festivities in the British Isles. However, under Elizabeth I the children of the Chapel Royal took part in Shrove Monday and Tuesday masques and today there are still towns and villages which faithfully maintain Shrove Tuesday customs such as street football where ancient rules take precedence over modern traffic laws. The pancake bell, which may be derived from a church bell announcing confession time, often now precedes a pancake race where contestants toss a pancake in a frying pan as they run.

Abroad it is more difficult to ignore Shrove Tuesday since this is usually the climax of several days of carnival involving not just processions of floats but days off with much dressing up as clowns or other characters. In his 1818 poem *Beppo*, Byron notes that abroad

Some weeks before Shrove Tuesday comes about
The people take their fill of recreation.

In Spain carnival was quickly rediscovered, starting in San Roque in Cadiz, following the return of democracy. Some processions, especially in Germany, have giant caricatures of political figures. Venice, Rio, New Orleans and Port of Spain are famous for their carnivals. The word *carnival* is derived from the Latin *carne vale* meaning *farewell to meat*. In France and New Orleans today is called *Mardi Gras* meaning *Fat Tuesday*. Gianduiotti, the small gold wrapped ground hazelnut chocolate like an upturned boat, was first made to be eaten during Turin's 1865 pre-Lent carnival. Sadly the Nice carnival has become so big that it sometimes ignores the inconvenient calendar and continues into Lent.

In 1559 Pieter Bruegel the Elder painted *The Fight Between Carnival and Lent* which shows the tension between the extremes of carnival and Lent.

Pancakes are part of both Candlemas and Shrove Tuesday in France. In Galicia pancakes are eaten at the end of meals during the week before Lent. Pancakes are also a central feature of Russia's pre-Lent week, called Maslenitsa, which ends on a Sunday. Swedes enjoy cream buns called *selma* with an almond, cardamom and marzipan filling. Poles, who started the countdown to Lent on Fat Thursday last week by eating doughnuts, finish today with pancakes.

SHROVE TUESDAY EVENTS

Pancake Races

Olney

The Buckinghamshire town of Olney, pronounced *owney*, claims to have invented the pancake race in 1445. The female competitors wearing aprons and each carrying a frying pan gather outside the Market Place by the Pancake Race Start plaque. At 11.55am the churchwardens start the race during which pancakes must be tossed twice over the 450 yards to the church. The winner is greeted in Churchyard Lane by the vicar saying the words 'The peace of the Lord be always with you' and by the verger. Immediately afterwards in church, where the pans are piled round the font, there is an ecumenical Shriving Service. Hymns include *Amazing Grace*, written in 1772 by Olney curate John Newton.

City of London

Since 2004 the Inter-Livery Pancake Race has been held in Guildhall Yard where lemons are provided by the Fruiterers' Company, eggs by the Poulters', forks by the Cutlers', gloves by the Glovers' whilst the Gunmakers' Company starts the heats with a cannon. The event begins with a prayer and contestants wear livery robes.

Southwark, London

The race which started in 2007 is held in Borough Market where the Dean of Southwark starts the heats and presents the trophy.

Wimborne, Dorset

The race around the outside of Wimborne Minster was revived in 1998 having lapsed for sixteen years. Competitors include school children, teachers, other adults and people in wheelchairs. After the clock has struck at 11am, a bell is rung from the tower and the races, which require the tossing a pancake at the four corners of the church, are started by the town crier.

Westminster, London

The Pancake Greaze takes place at 11am in Westminster School. The dean's verger, dean and chapter, the head master and school chef, holding a pan of two pancakes, form a procession in the abbey cloister and make their way to the school hall, known as Up School. Pancakes, which include horsehair and Polyfilla to strengthen them, are tossed by the chef over a high bar. A violent tussle for a piece involving around forty boys follows for several minutes. Pancake scraps are weighed and the boy with the heaviest receives a George IV sovereign. The coin is exchanged for a £5 note. The custom, which dates from at least 1753 and was witnessed by reformer Jeremy Bentham, no longer has such a packed and expectant audience as it is now webcast.

But the Greaze remains a school only occasion unlike the public Parliamentary Pancake Race begun in 1997 and held in nearby Victoria Tower Gardens.

Pancake Bells
At Richmond in Yorkshire, the Holy Trinity Chapel bell, once rung daily at 6am to wake apprentices, is rung today at 10.55am. A bell at Newark parish church is rung at 11am for ten minutes. In the past, the youngest ringer was paid one shilling for the task. Cirencester's church tolls its ninth bell at noon for fifteen minutes.

At Toddington in Bedfordshire the church bell rings at noon as children from St George's School go behind the church to climb Conger Hill mound where they lie down and listen for a witch frying pancakes. The oldest written record of the event is 1865 when it is described as being an 'ancient custom'. *Conger* is derived from an old English word for *rabbit warren*.

Shrove Fair
Lichfield, Staffordshire
The Shrovetide Old Fair, dating from at least 1409 and confirmed by Royal Charter in 1623, once ran from 12 noon on Ash Wednesday to noon on Friday as a selling fair but by the 1870s it had become mainly a pleasure fair. And from 1890 until today it has been only that. The mayor and sheriff walk in procession from the Guildhall to the Market Square where at 12 noon the Town Crier reads a proclamation and the mayor opens the fair. As the church bell rings the civic party and children take a free ride on the roundabouts. This custom only dates from 1948. Afterwards there is another more recent addition –a male and a female pancake race is run along Bore Street where cattle were once sold during the Old Fair. The mayor's party returns to the Guildhall to toast the Queen and the Old Fair and enjoy a piece of Simnel cake (page 42) as served since at least 1747. The Old

Fair is the country's first fair of the year unless St Valentine's Day falls first (page 169).

Shrove Football
Alnwick

A football match between St Paul's and St Michael's parishes is played in The Pastures below the castle. Until 1827 this was a street game dating from at least 1762. At 2pm the inner gates of the castle swing open and the Duke of Northumberland climbs up to the battlements to throw the ball down to the crowd. The Duke's Piper, playing the distinctive Northumberland pipes, leads the crowd of about two hundred, mainly children and young people, down The Peth and across the Lion Bridge to a kissing gate at The Pastures. Here two hales (ten foot high arches of greenery for goals) have been set up. The game starts at 2.30pm with the blowing of a horn and ends about 4pm or earlier if a team scores two hales. Any number of people can join the two teams. Five hundred took part in 1886 and in the 1980s teams were about 50 strong but the figure has grown again. After the prize-giving, the ball is thrown up and whoever gets it across the River Aln keeps it. This usually involves much struggling in the river, which sometimes still has ice on it.

Ashbourne

Royal Shrovetide Football is played in and around the Derbyshire village of Ashbourne. After the singing of *Auld Lang Syne* and the national anthem at 2pm, a leather ball is thrown to an always very large crowd made up of Up'ards, those born on the north side of Henmore Brook, and Down'ards born on the south side. The goals are three miles apart on the site of mills in Sturston and Clifton. The painted ball, blessed in St Oswald's Church on the last Sunday before Lent, can be kicked or carried and, since it is filled with cork, will float when dropped in the stream. The game ends when two goals have been scored, or at 10pm. The earliest record of the game is 1683 although it is claimed as much older. The last legal challenge to the mayhem was in 1891 when people were fined for playing in the street. Since about 1859 the game has been repeated on Ash Wednesday. The Royal prefix dates from 1922 when Princess Mary married on Shrove Tuesday, but the Prince of Wales (Edward VIII) turned up (i.e. threw) the ball in 1928, and the present Prince of Wales followed his great uncle in 2003 when 8000 people packed into the village on Ash Wednesday. Others who have turned up the ball include Matthew Parris in 1984 when he was the local MP.

Atherstone

The Atherstone Ball Game, allegedly dating from 1199 but only documented from 1790, is played in Long Street on the line of the Roman Watling Street. The ball is a 27-inch diameter water-filled leather version made by rugby football manufacturer Gilbert of Rugby. Shops are boarded up for the 3pm start when the ball is thrown by a celebrity from an upstairs window of Barclays bank. Past guests include George Formby, Larry Grayson and Ken Dodd. The at-first friendly football game, with children and pensioners allowed a go, has only a few rules which were revised in 2012. The light ball soars above the buildings and sometimes becomes stuck in windows or an alley. After 4.30pm the game becomes more competitive and rough with the ball sometimes deflated. The winner is the person holding the ball when a klaxon sounds at 5pm. At least 3000 people throng Long Street. Until recently it was also traditional for children to 'attack' visitors and onlookers with pea-shooters. The football is preceded by pancake races.

Sedgefield

Street football takes place all afternoon at Sedgefield. The first record of the game is 1802, but it is said to have begun in 1246 when tradesmen working on the church tower tossed a ball through a window to farmers below. On the green there is a ring in the ground, for tethering horses, known as the bull ring. At 1pm a small ball is passed three times through the ring and thrown in the air. The crowd of around two hundred young people kick and throw the ball around nearby streets. Shop windows are boarded up. Number 5 in the main street has frames of chicken wire which during the rest of the year double up as pond covering and tomato plant frames. The owner devised the frames after once being called from work to find a policeman guarding the ball inside his front room from an angry crowd. There is no known organiser so that no one can be held responsible for any damage. The ball, once provided by the parish church and made of leather by the blacksmith, is now a hockey ball covered in leather by a saddler. By a mysterious arrangement the ball occasionally disappears in a car and then returns about an hour later.

The two goals, called alleys, were a pond (now covered by two bungalows next to North End Garage) and a stream so now the climax comes at 5pm or a little earlier when the ball is 'alleyed' into the stream, the one goal, and brought back to be passed through the bull ring. The person who does this is the winner and keeps the ball. The Iceton family has five balls dating from 1880.

There is low key policing and no interference with what appears to be mayhem as people scatter and traffic is halted. Villagers strongly defend the tradition and the numbers taking part always rises from around 200 to 300 when Shrove Tuesday falls during the half-term holiday – although some teenagers take the day off school anyway. There is a pause in the rough play if the ball is passed to a child or older person.

Corfe Castle

Corfe has a nominal football kickabout. In accordance with a custom first recorded in 1651, the church bell is rung at noon to call members of the Ancient Order of Purbeck Marblers and Stonecutters to gather at The Fox. The last man to be married brings the football 'according to the custom of our company'. At 12.30pm they cross the road for their annual meeting in Britain's smallest Town Hall. New apprentices arrive with the nearest equivalent to 'a quart of beer, a penny loaf and 6/8d'. At 1.30pm about ten younger members emerge to kick the football up West Street and then along a passage on to Middle Halves, once used for strip farming land. They return to the The Fox at about 2pm. This is the remnant of the pre-1860 custom of dribbling the ball to Ower Quay, a loading point for stone dating from 1250. The three-mile route was along Peppercorn Lane which recalls the 1lb of pepper once presented with the football to the Ower Farm tenant to preserve the right of way. In 1992 a new police officer, unaware of the tradition, attempted to stop the football being kicked along the road in Corfe.

Hurling the Silver Ball

Hurling the Silver Ball, a once widespread Cornish game with few rules, starts with calling up the ball at 4.15pm opposite the church lychgate in St Columb Major. The crowd is at least fifty-strong. The ball, the size of a cricket ball and made from applewood coated with silver, is thrown up at 4.30pm in the market square. Teams from Town and Country struggle to carry the ball to either the Town or Country goals in the form of ancient stones two miles apart. For the first hour the ball remains in the boarded-up town with about thirty mainly males chasing it up and down the long main street. Occasionally there is a pause to hand the ball to a young or old person or even take it indoors for a sick person to briefly hold. The game ends as soon as a goal has been scored or the ball carried across the parish boundary but it must end by 8pm when the winning scorer has to call up the ball in the square. Afterwards, at The Ring of Bells pub, the ball is dropped into a jug of cocoa and 'silver cocoa' is served to around eight children who bring mugs. This recalls the brief Puritan period when drink was frowned on. Afterwards the scorer tours the pubs dipping the ball into jugs of beer to make 'silver beer'. The earliest record of the custom is 1594 when the churchwardens' accounts mention payment for a silver ball. Since the early eighteenth century the game has also been played on the second Saturday of Lent. As few as twenty-five people might be present for the final calling up the ball but more people take part in the second game. The town logo is a hand holding the silver ball with the motto 'Do your best' and appears on school sweatshirts.

Skipping

In Scarborough today there is a half-day holiday for schools allowing young and old go to the seafront for skipping. During the nineteenth century, apprentices and servants gathered on the South Bay front for their Shrove Tuesday holiday when they played with balls bought at the fair. The skipping tradition only started about 1903 when fishermen repairing nets for the new season lent ropes to the school children. Foreshore Road is closed to traffic and by 1.30pm it is crowded with children enthusiastically skipping with long ropes. A bell above a shop, on the corner of North Street and Westborough, is rung by the mayor at noon prior to a pancake race.

Shroving

Shroving involved knocking on doors and asking for money in return for a song or poem. Any refusing to give might have broken crockery thrown at their door. Durweston, a Dorset village which has its own Christmas carols, maintains the last example of the custom recorded in 1831 by poet William Barnes. In 1925 villager Valentine Rickman left money to ensure that children would each receive twelve pence for Shroving. Since 1993 it has been the custom for the children to sing the rhyme outside the cottages and give out flowers rather than receive money. Children assemble outside the school at 9.30am and sing the rhyme known to Barnes: 'We become a'shroving for a piece of pancake,/ Or a bit of bacon,/Or a little truckle cheese of your own making,/ Blow the fire and het the pot,/For we've have come a'shroving.' Then the school divides into two groups to tour the village. After an hour the older group returns by way of the churchyard to lay flowers on Rickman's grave. Shroving does not take place if today falls during the half-term holiday.

Tip Toeing

Tip Toeing takes place in Gittisham soon after the school bus returns to the largely thatched Devon village, described as the 'ideal village' by Prince Charles. The WI serves tea in the hall at 4pm before about ten children set out in two teams: the Little Ones who stay in the village and the Big Ones who go out to farms. The children, carrying the group's money box, stop outside houses to chant: 'Tip tip toe/Please for a penny and then we'll go!' The origin may have been to collect money to buy ingredients for making pancakes. Householders tend to be ready with sweets and crisps as well as coins. Now the modest amount of money collected is divided amongst the participants and any children too ill to take part. Each child receives about £6.50. If today falls during the half-term holiday then the custom is observed a little earlier in the afternoon. When the village had a school it started at 10am.

Procession

In London the Stationers' Company walk in procession from Stationers' Hall to nearby St Paul's Cathedral for a service in the crypt at 11.15am. The preacher receives ten shillings (50p) for the sermon and afterwards the robed livery returns for a buffet lunch known as 'cakes and ale'. The phrase is more associated with post Easter revels (see page 154). Since 2005 the route has been by way of Paternoster Square and the relocated Temple Bar. But until 2016 the event was on Ash Wednesday because of an 1612 endowment requirement. The reason remains a mystery but after two hundred years cathedral and livery agreed that today was more suitable for a celebratory refreshment than the first day of Lent.

Carnival

Binche, Belgium

The origin of the word *binge* is *Binche* in Belgium where its carnival dates from the late fourteenth century. In 2003, the event was recognised by UNESCO as a 'masterpiece of oral and intangible patrimony of humanity'. This afternoon at about 3pm there is a parade in the Grande Place of a thousand Gilles, male inhabitants, in straw stuffed costumes who throw 300,000 Spanish oranges. Each Gille carries a short broom to drive out winter and has a personal drummer contributing to a familiar rhythmic beat. The

Gilles tradition dates from before 1795 and their costume is fusion of Gilles and Pierrot derived from the Comédie Italienne. The oranges, representing the coming of spring, replaced flour in the 1830s. The Gilles' have worn identical masks since the late 1850s after which faces were no longer whitened by flour. The day ends with a flame-lit parade and fireworks.

Cologne, Germany

Carnival began last Thursday with Women's Carnival Day when women may kiss any man. The big parade with horses and bands, taking four hours to pass, is on Rose Monday (dating from 1823) and follows a route from St Gereon to St Severin via the cathedral. Huge papier-maché figures lampoon politicians. Today other parades are in the residential suburbs. As the city of the Magi there is no King of the Carnival, but a prince. The carnival tradition dates from 1277.

Ivrea, Italy

At Ivrea near Turin the feature of carnival is, like Binche, also oranges, but here it involves throwing them on a massive scale. The fruit is brought from Sicily. Today is the climax to the carnival which began at 2.30pm on Thursday with a proclamation handing over mayoral power to a Napoleonic carnival 'General'. In 1808 the local carnivals were amalgamated by the Napoleonic government. At 9pm on Saturday the chosen 'pretty miller's daughter' appears on the Town Hall balcony. This recalls 1194 when a miller's daughter rebelled against the lord and despot and since 1858 a young Mugnaia (miller's daughter) character has been carnival queen. In processions she throws chocolates and mimosa to the crowds from her carriage whilst costumed teams throw oranges representing stones hurled at the despot's castle. The orange element began with the throwing of oranges from balconies in the early nineteenth century and some suggest that the oranges are really a replacement for eggs thrown in fun before the start of Lent. The medieval cobbled streets of the walled town become thick with over a million mashed oranges.

Today's procession starts at 2pm with the final orange-throwing sessions at four centres including the main squares. At 8pm *scarli*, tall poles covered in greenery, are burned in various districts with the main scarli set alight outside the Town Hall at 10pm. This symbolises both the despot's castle burning and the end of carnival. At 10.15pm pipers lead the way to the burning of the last scarlo which is in the San Grato parish. A lone piper and drummers play a funeral march. Afterwards, with pipes and drums playing, everyone embraces saying 'Goodbye until Thursday at one' meaning 'See you next year'.

Venice, Italy
Today is called Martedì Grasso (Fat Tuesday). The Carnevale, dating from 1296, reached its zenith of bad behaviour in the eighteenth century, but died out after the Venetian Republic fell in 1797. Restoration as an annual occasion was in 1980. Last Friday's open-air masked ball in St Mark's Square is the heart of the programme. Today, the twelve days climax with a firework display and music enjoyed by around 55,000 people, some wearing masks, and the tolling of bells at midnight to announce Lent.

Viareggio, Italy
The carnival started as a one day event on Sunday in 1873 but today it is the leading Italian carnival known for large cartoon figures of famous people.

New Orleans, USA
Mardi Gras arrived with the French settlers in the 1700s. The first floats were first seen in 1857 and now there are over sixty processions organised by krewes (or clubs) with around five hundred sponsored floats. Individuals on floats are kept busy throwing plastic beads, sweets and other gifts into the crowds. In and around Bourbon Street there are people in exotic costumes and plenty of free jazz. This is now claimed as the biggest party in the world with the daily parades from last Wednesday building

up to nine from 8am today. Still on sale are King Cakes which first appear at Epiphany decorated with the yellow, green and purple colours of Mardi Gras.

Rio de Janeiro, Brazil
This, the biggest carnival with at least 370,000 visitors, begins on Friday and is a five day spectacular of parades and dancing. The first parade of floats was in 1786 and the samba parade started in the 1930s. Now months of preparation go into getting the fourteen huge samba schools rehearsed for a themed competitive parade of dance and floats from Saturday to Tuesday nights in the specially built Sambódromo. The floats feature young girls hoping to be seen on live television and launch a show business career. However, this has not taken carnival off the streets as there are numerous informal rule-free costumed dances around the city. In the heat and exuberance there is a trend for some female dancers to perform topless. In 2001 the Archbishop of Rio urged people to go to confession rather than dress up in scanty costumes. Carnival has been marred by deaths; one hundred and twenty people died in 1981, and in 2010 the mayor tried to limit bad behaviour. Carnivals in Recife and Olinda remain more authentic.

Port of Spain, Trinidad
A three-day carnival enjoyed by French settlers started in the late eighteenth century and from 1834 freed black slaves joined in. After 1843 it was agreed that carnival should be reduced to two days to avoid Sunday. Today the weekend is given over to more sober fetes and just after midnight on Sunday there is the informal start known as *Jouvert* from *jour overt* meaning *start of the day*. Revellers cover themselves and others in mud or chocolate and dance to dawn. Today Carnival Tuesday is the main day with exuberant dancing in the streets until midnight. Buying or making costumes is known as 'playing the mas'.

LENT

Ash Wednesday

Today is the first day of Lent. The English name for Lent comes from the Saxon *lencten* meaning *lengthen* as this is the time of the year when days get longer. The name Ash comes from the ashes received on the head in church today. Ashes, a symbol of mourning and penitence since Old Testament times, have been a feature of the start of Lent since the eighth century. It is a remnant of 'sackcloth and ashes' worn in early days to acknowledge repentance and unworthiness.

The contrast with yesterday has long been striking. 'The Christians go mad but thanks to ashes that the Church puts on their heads they come to their senses and are cured of their madness,' commented the Turkish ambassador to Rome in the 1690s.

The Forty Days of Lent

Lent is a period of about forty days during which preparation can be made to observe the climax of Holy Week and celebrate the resurrection of Jesus on Easter Day.

It is customary to keep this period by both giving up something and by trying to examine and renew oneself. Self-denial and self-control keep one from the blindness of over-indulgence, helping us to associate with Christ's sufferings, focus on belief and remember others who have difficult lives. It also reminds us of our dependence on God.

Pope Pius V refused to ban chocolate in Lent 1569 as he considered a cup of hot chocolate too disgusting to be enjoyable. But giving up chocolate has much to commend it, if only to make a chocolate egg at Easter special. Although some Belgian beers were originally brewed as 'liquid bread' to sustain the body in Lent there is a tendency today to refrain from alcohol.

We can also give money and/or time to a good cause. St Theodulph, who wrote the hymn sung on Palm Sunday (page 57), suggested that the forty days of Lent is the tithe or, tenth of the year, given to God.

St John Paul II, speaking as Pope in 1979, said that going without things in Lent does not only consist of giving away what we do not need. 'Going without things is to free oneself from the slavery of a civilisation that is always urging people on to greater comfort and consumption, without a thought for the preservation of our environment which is the common heritage of humanity.'

It may also be a time when we should do something for ourselves, such as rest or tidy our affairs, so that we are better equipped to help others. 'How can you draw close to God when you are far from your own self?' asked St Augustine of Hippo.

Lent was in existence by 325 when the Council of Nicea met (in today's Turkey) and recorded the forty-day period. Forty is a popular round figure in the Bible. Noah endured a forty day flood, Moses spent forty days on Mount Sinai and Jesus fasted in the desert for forty days.

It is forty days from today to Easter Eve if we omit Sundays which always mark the resurrection of Christ. This is why the six-week period starts on a Wednesday. However, the Sundays during Lent do have a Lenten feel and should not be used as an excuse to break any abstinence.

In Milan, where the Ambrosian Rite is used, Sundays are considered part of Lent so Lent begins next Sunday allowing the Ambrosian Carnival to end on *Sabato Grasso* or Fat Saturday instead of Fat Tuesday.

Fast Day

Today, like Good Friday, is a day of fasting and abstinence meaning that one should have one main meal with no snacking (fast) and refrain from eating meat (abstinence).

Early Christians maintained the Jewish custom of refraining

from certain meats which were feast day food. Fasting without show with fellow believers engenders a sense of solidarity. It is an expression of faith, making one more sensitive to the needs of others and leaving spare money for helping others.

Fasting and abstinence should be observed by adults in good health aged 18 to 60. Those aged 14 to 17 should follow the abstinence rule.

Abstinence is observed every Friday.

In the Bible
Matthew 6.1-6 and Matthew 4.1-11; Mark 1.12-15 and Luke 4.1-13
Jesus' advice on giving, praying and fasting is to do so in an unostentatious manner.

He spent forty days fasting in arid territory resisting temptation.

In Church
There are now no flowers in churches. Vestments are purple. The opening penitential rite and the Gloria are omitted and the word Alleluia, meaning *praise God*, is prohibited until Easter.

The Old Testament and gospel readings feature fasting.

An alternative to the Psalm 50 responsorial psalm said or sung between the first two readings is the Lent Prose, *Attende Domine*, derived from the Mozarabic breviary. The refain was written in 1895 by Dom Joseph Pothier at Solesmes Abbey in France and only made popular when the translation was broadcast by the BBC in 1934:

> *Hear us, O Lord, have mercy upon us:*
> *for we have sinned against thee.*
> *(Attende, Domine, et miserere:*
> *quia peccavimus tibi.)*

After the sermon there is the opportunity to go up to the sanctuary and have the sign of the cross made with ashes on the forehead (like the cross in baptism) to outwardly express penance and repentance. (The ashes are made from burning last year's Palm Sunday palm crosses; see page 57.) The priest, making the mark, says: 'Remember that you are dust and to dust you will return, turn away from sin and be faithful to the Gospel' or 'Turn away from sin and hear the good news'. The reference to dust is based on Genesis 2.7 and 3.19. Our bodies will one day be dust in the ground but by receiving ash on our heads we acknowledge God as creator and remind ourselves that we are flesh which will die although our spirit is immortal.

The Roman Catholic gospel reading, and sometimes the Anglican one, suggests that we should avoid any outer sign of fasting or prayer (Matthew 6.1-6, 16-18). But today it is understood that having a smudge on the forehead can be a visible witness of being a Christian observing Lent, awaken faith in the hearts of others or start a conversation. This happens after lunchtime services in the City of London. Carol Monaghan MP, appearing at a House of Commons committee, declined a suggestion that she might wish to remove the cross on her head because television cameras were present. However, some countries such as Italy maintain the ancient custom of scattering ashes on the head which leaves a less visible mark.

Suitable hymns include *Forty Days and Forty Nights*, a poem by George Smyttan when rector of Hawksworth in Nottinghamshire and published in *The Penny Post* in 1856, which looks to 'Eastertide'. *Dear Lord and Father of mankind* requests forgiveness of 'foolish ways'.

Sometimes the choir might sing Allegri's *The Miserere* which will be heard again on Good Friday (see page 86).

Although today sees churches well attended it is not a holy day of obligation. Ashing can be part of a liturgy of the word service without the Eucharist which allows for ecumenical participation.

Ash Wednesday Observances

Spain

This evening sees a carnival farewell known as the Burial of the Sardine. In Madrid, where the custom was recorded by Goya, the procession with bands sets out at 6pm from the Church of San Antonio de la Florida, where the artist is buried below his frescoes. After a slow tour of the district, the mock funeral party, organised by the Happy Confraternity of the Burial of the Sardine, reaches Casa de Campo parkland about 9.30pm. Many people, singing songs about the wonderful sardine, wear black and carry tiny open coffins containing a sardine. This satirical lament for carnival may have its origin in the late eighteenth century when Carlos III ordered a shipload of rotting sardines to be buried. But the custom also symbolises the burial of the past to allow for transformation. Other smaller processions take place in other parts of the capital.

In both Alicante and Arrecife in Lanzarote a large papier-mâché fish is burnt as 'widows' wail and in Santona, Cantabria, there has since 1981 been the Burial of the Sea Bream which involves a raft set alight at sea.

The Burial of the Sardine can be compared with England's pre-Reformation custom of Burying the Alleluia before Lent which involved choirboys burying a coffin after Vespers to mark the end of singing Alleluia until Easter when the box would be dug up.

Ivrea, Italy

In Ivrea (see Shrove Tuesday above) there is a 'marmalade-like' smell as the streets are hosed down to remove of the last traces of the oranges thrown. From 10am people queue in the Piazza Lamarmora with dishes and basins to collect fried cod and polenta which is cooked in vast vats. This traditional food is also served in cafés and restaurants.

Rome

The Pope goes in the late afternoon to the church on Rome's Aventine Hill dedicated to St Anselm, Archbishop of Canterbury.

From the church there is a penitential procession to Santa Sabina, part of the Dominicans' headquarters.

A litany, longer but similar to the one heard at the Easter Vigil (see page 93), is sung as the procession divides round the St Anselm cloister and moves down the narrow street. Familiar saints invoked include St Agnes and St Thomas Becket. Taking part with the Pope are cardinals, archbishops, bishops, the Benedictine monks of St Anselm's and the Dominicans of Santa Sabina. His Holiness, in a tradition more than a thousand years old and re-established by Pope John XXIII, celebrates Mass. Santa Sabina's fifth-century wooden entrance door has the oldest representation of Christ on the Cross.

First Sunday of Lent

There is a distinctly different feel to the liturgy compared to last Sunday.

In Church

Where there is a choral tradition, such as at Truro Cathedral, the Mass may be preceded by the singing of The Litany in procession. Vestments continue to be purple and there are no flowers. The Gloria and Alleluia are both omitted.

It may also start with the priest sprinkling the congregation with holy water instead of the usual penitential rite as a reminder of baptism for which many are preparing at Easter.

Every third year (2018, 2021, etc.) the readings have the theme of water and baptism with the story of Noah in the first reading taken up in the second reading by St Paul who sees the flood as water of baptism cleansing us from our sins.

The gospel reading is (except in every third year; see above) an account of Jesus' forty days of resisting temptation and fasting in the wilderness, which makes a connection with the forty days of Lent having just begun.

The responsorial psalm every third year is Psalm 50 as on Ash Wednesday although in the Anglican Church it can often remain the Lent Prose (see page 33) for all Lent Sundays.

Suitable hymns are *Water of life* and *Forty days and forty nights*.

Second Friday of Lent
CAFOD Lent Fast Day

Today is CAFOD Lent Fast Day. Christians are asked to forgo a main meal and donate the cost to the poor via the Catholic Agency for Overseas Development.

The first CAFOD Lent Fast Day, called Family Fast Day, was held in 1957 in Austria at the instigation of Elizabeth von Strachotinsky, the country's representative of the World Union of Catholic Women's Organisations, who had heard the director general of the Food and Agricultural Organisation Shri Binay Ranjan Sen speak about hunger and malnutrition in the developing world.

Jacqueline Stuyt-Simpson, the World Union's UK representative, put the idea to Britain's Catholic Women's League and Union of Catholic Mothers who organised a British Family Fast Day in 1960. The event was so successful that it was repeated and in 1962 the Roman Catholic Bishops of England and Wales set up CAFOD to provide a focus for all small charitable efforts which were already taking place and to promote the Family Fast Day.

CAFOD works alongside Christian Aid to build a world without hunger and war by putting faith into action.

Second Sunday of Lent

In Church

The gospel reading in Roman Catholic churches is an account of the Transfiguration (see page 14). A suitable hymn is *Tis good, Lord, to be here!*.

Fourth Sunday of Lent

Mothering Sunday
Laetare Sunday
Mid-Lent Sunday
Refreshment Sunday
Rose Sunday

Mothering Sunday

Today is known as Mothering Sunday only in the British Isles, Nigeria and some Anglican churches in the Commonwealth. Children, including adult sons and daughters, send cards and give flowers to their mothers.

For over three centuries until the late twentieth century, in both the Anglican Church and Roman Catholic Church, the first reading at Mass had a mother image: 'Jerusalem ... which is the mother of us all' (St Paul's Letter to Galatians 4.26). The KJV gospel was the Feeding of the 5000 (John 6.1) which gave the excuse for the mid-Lent modest feasting.

This original 'mother' theme was extended from Jerusalem to the 'mother' church – the cathedral or the parish church – that might have had jurisdiction over nearby chapels or village churches, and which it became traditional to visit in mid-Lent. When village congregations visited the nearby mother church, maybe in the town, older children would have met up with their mothers. So mothers of children were embraced in the mother theme from the 1600s. Also young people in domestic service were allowed a home visit six months after being hired at autumn fairs. This became known as going 'a mothering' or 'mid-Lenting'. Walking home they would pick wild flowers for their mother.

In 1644, Royalist soldier Richard Symonds wrote in his diary: 'Every Midlent Sunday is a great day at Worcester, when all the children and godchildren meet at the head and cheife of the family and have a feast. They call it the Mothering-day.'

On mid-Lent Sunday 1870 curate Francis Kilvert's diary, written near Hay-on-Wye, records: 'All the country is in an upturn going out visiting. Girls and boys going home to see their mothers and taking them cakes, brothers and sisters of middle age to see each other. It is a grand visiting day.'

Mothering Sunday and Mother's Day

Mothering Sunday has largely given way to Mother's Day after the secular Mother's Day observed in some countries in May. The May custom, begun in the USA in 1908, is now followed in Canada, Australia and Germany. Britain's Mothering Sunday custom owes much to US soldiers who brought Mother's Day with them when stationed in Britain during World War II.

In 1913 Constance Penswick Smith had realised that the American Mother's Day could supersede the little-observed Mothering Sunday. She promoted the traditional day in Coddington, Nottinghamshire, where her father had been vicar and the village sign now depicts her. Later at St Cyprian's Church in Nottingham she founded, with her friend Ellen Porter, The Society for the Observance of Mothering Sunday. Constance designed cards, wrote special hymns and encouraged the making of posies. Violets were more common then than daffodils. In 1921 she published a book, *Mothering Sunday*, and as a result Mothering Sunday had a strong hold in the Southwell Diocese between the two World Wars.

Elsewhere Mothering Sunday traditions began to die out although the customs were still properly observed at St Magnus Church in the City of London as late as the 1930s. There in the morning individual Simnel cakes were blessed and distributed to children and in the afternoon rector Henry Fynes-Clinton led a devotional visit to St Paul's Cathedral, the mother church.

Clypping

Some parishes maintain the custom of clypping, or clipping, the church. The congregation goes out into the churchyard to join hands and encircle the church. This hugging of the building, often the main or mother church, symbolises love for the church. Shakespeare uses the word *clip*, meaning *surround* or *encompass*, in *Othello* (Act 3, scene 3) where Iago says: 'You elements, that clip us round about.'

Simnel Cake

Children returning home were sometimes given a piece of cake and this may be the origin of the Simnel cake. According to a Shropshire legend the name comes from brother and sister Simon and Nell, who tried to make a cake for their mother. A scratch-relief in All Saints, Leighton Buzzard showing a woman with a spoon pulling a man's ear, is said to represent Nell and Simon. However, the cake's origin can be traced back to at least 1042 in Winchester. A *simnellus* was a fine wheaten loaf baked on special occasions using flour called simila. This bread slowly developed into the round fruitcake with marzipan topping. Sometimes mothers kept their slice of cake until Easter when many now enjoy a Simnel cake.

'I'll to thee a simnell bring/Gainst thou go a-mothering,' wrote Robert Herrick in 1648.

Most Simnel cakes are made to the Shrewsbury recipe and sometimes with a crown of twelve marzipan balls representing the Apostles or eleven if omitting Judas (see page 66). Lancashire's Bury Simnel is a flat spiced cake resembling a rock cake. In Wiltshire the Devizes Simnel is star-shaped.

Laetare Sunday

Laetare Sunday, once the more widely used name for today, comes from the entrance antiphon at the start of Mass: *Laetare Jerusalem* meaning *Rejoice Jerusalem* (Isaiah 66.10-11). This likens Jerusalem to a mother: 'Rejoice, Jerusalem, and all who love her. Be joyful, all who were in mourning: exult and be satisfied at her consoling breast.'

The church building will become Jerusalem in two weeks when, as part of the Palm procession, the congregation enters the church to observe Holy Week. The joy of mid-Lent Sunday is the anticipation of Easter with a brief glimpse of colour. Abroad, where Mother's Day is on another date (see page 41), the name Laetare remains familiar. Some Belgium towns have Laetare carnivals today.

In Church

The introduction to the Mass has the mother theme (see above). Flowers are allowed – there is often a blessing of posies which are distributed to children who present them to their mothers. The Anglican Common Worship provides special collect and readings which can be used instead of those for the Fourth Sunday.

The Anglican gospel readings maintain the mother theme with Simeon's warning to Mary of difficult times to come for her son Jesus (Luke 2.33-35) and the crucifixion of her son (John 19.25-27). An alternative first reading is the story of Moses in the bulrushes (Exodus 2.1-10). It is a reminder that, as many mothers know, the privilege of motherhood can also involve anguish.

Common Worship's post-Communion prayer reflects the ancient Roman introit: '... as a mother feeds her children at the breast you feed us ...'.

Rose vestments can be worn in a tradition which highlights the day. Rose is a mixture Lent purple and Easter white.

Today's hymns sometimes have a Marian theme and might include *Sing we of the Blessed Mother*, *Jesus, good above all other* and *Her Virgin eyes saw God incarnate born*. There can be a Christmas feel with *Jesus, good above all other*. Timothy Dudley-Smith wrote *Our Father God in Heaven* specially for Mothering Sunday. If there is clypping afterwards then a suitable hymn is *We love the place, O God* which is based on Psalm 26.8: 'Lord, I have loved the habitation of thy house; and the place where thine honour dwelleth.'

Mothering Sunday Customs

Clypping

At Staplehurst in Kent the clypping ceremony has taken place since 1950 when it was thought to be the only church maintaining the custom. After the sermon the choir leads the congregation twice anti-clockwise round the outside of the church as bells peal. On returning to the west door the peace is exchanged with the clergy and churchwardens.

After the parish Eucharist at Cookham Dean in Berkshire, the vicar leads the members of the congregation with hands linked anti-clockwise round the outside of the church. Once it is surrounded ,all face the building and raise hands to shout 'hosanna!'. The custom was introduced by in 1972.

At All Saints Church Coddington in Nottinghamshire, where Constance Smith is buried, an afternoon service embraces all traditions – presentation of flowers, clypping and Simnel cake afterwards. During the clypping, the congregation sings *We love the place, O God*.

Carnival

Laetare carnival at Stavelot in Belgium dates from 1502. A huge procession in the afternoon features white hooded figures with long red nose masks throwing confetti. Cannons also shoot confetti at the crowds and first-floor flats. The long nose tradition dates from 1502 when monks were banned from the procession and so others donned white costumes and masks. Around 35,000 people watch the 2000 participants.

Fosses-la-Ville (see page 159) also has an afternoon carnival. Here the street procession features Chinels (pulcinella-style costumes), music, dancing and stilt walkers.

Fifth Sunday of Lent

Passion Sunday
Carlin Sunday

The Fifth Sunday of Lent marks the beginning of Passiontide. *Passion*, from the Latin *passio* meaning *suffering*, refers to the last six days of Christ's life on earth in Jerusalem from Palm Sunday.

Lent now moves into real time as it becomes possible to plot the last days of Jesus' ministry. He makes his way to Jerusalem with twelve main disciples to keep the Passover. We know that Jesus had recently been at Bethany near Jerusalem, where he raised Lazarus from his tomb. In a few days, maybe Friday, Jesus and his followers will be at Jericho where on the outskirts he heals a blind man called Bartimaeus. There Jesus stays with tax gatherer Zaccheus who had climbed into a sycamore tree for a better view of the visiting preacher drawing an expectant crowd. On Saturday Jesus and his disciples will be back at Bethany.

In Church

From today until Easter many churches maintain the tradition of veiling statues and crosses in purple to help concentrate minds on the events leading up to Christ's crucifixion and resurrection. A huge cloth is thrown over the statue of St Peter at the back of Westminster Cathedral and even the glass tomb of St John Southworth is covered.

Today's gospel reading in some years (2020, 2023) can recall Jesus' raising of Lazarus when his action and teaching, hinting of his own imminent death and resurrection, won support but also came to the notice of the Jerusalem authorities. It is a preview of Holy Week and its theme of death, life and joy.

Carlin Sunday Custom

In the north-east of England today is often known as Carlin, Carling or even Care Sunday. The name may derive from the word *care* meaning *mourning* and refer to the death of Christ. This week is sometimes known as Care Week. A still remembered rhyme naming Sundays from the second in Lent to Easter Day is: 'Tid, mid, miseray, Carlings, Palm and Pace-Egg Day.' *Miseray* is probably derived from the opening of Psalm 51 *Miserere mei* (see page 86).

Carlin also refers to black maple peas, carlings or carlins, which are grown in the UK and eaten today in parts of the North-East between the Berwick area on the Scottish Borders and Great Driffield in Yorkshire to the south. Carlin plants have pink and lilac flowers and reach around five feet high. There are two varieties: Black Badger and Red Fox.

The plants grew in monastery gardens but the origin of the custom is unknown. Some claim that it lies in one of the Scottish sieges of Newcastle and most probably in 1327 when Robert the Bruce besieged the town. Relief came on Passion Sunday when a Norwegian ship laden with carlins evaded the blockade to deliver peas to the starving population.

Cookery writer Jane Grigson, who was brought up in Sunderland, suggested that 'towards the end of winter, when stores ran low and famine came closer in, people shared the fodder put aside for animals'. Some of the newly dried harvest of peas would have been cooked around All Souls' Day in November with the remaining bulk stored to be used up in Lent.

The Carlin Sunday habit was spread in the nineteenth and twentieth centuries by those moving to new mining communities, and it remained strong in the 1950s. At Dalston and Durham there was also a tradition of using the dried peas in pea-shooters sometimes known as 'carlin shutters'.

Carlin peas are sold at this time of the year in Teesside, Durham, Durham County, Yorkshire and parts of Lancashire such as Bolton Market and as far west as Blackpool. Recently they have been promoted at Borough Market in London as 'a Lent food'.

At lunchtime today some public houses, in a custom dating from at least 1810, have saucers of carlins which are sometimes sprinkled with salt to increase thirst.

Carlins can be eaten with meat and vegetables, added to salad or even as a Lenten substitute for meat. The cooked peas last at least a week as another rhyme records:

> *Pease porridge hot,*
> *Pease porridge cold,*
> *Pease porridge in the pot*
> *Nine days old.*
> *Some like it hot,*
> *Some like it cold,*
> *Some like it in the pot*
> *Nine days old.*

Cooking guidelines: Soak half a pound (200g) of carlin peas in cold water overnight. Drain and place in a saucepan of boiling water. Boil for thirty minutes or until cooked but not mushy. Melt a little beef dripping or butter in a frying pan. A recent alternative to fat is vegetable oil. Drain the carlins and add to the pan. Fry for two to three minutes. Serve hot with salt, pepper and maybe vinegar. Some people add soft brown sugar and a drop of rum. Or leave to cool and eat as a snack with a drink.

HOLY WEEK

Saturday Before Palm Sunday

Holy Week starts tonight with evensong, vespers or Palm Sunday Vigil Mass as we live Jesus' last few days before the crucifixion in real time.

Holy Week
'Holy Week … is the peculiar privilege of Christians and should be their delight, their share in the sacred act of theatre, their most important week of all the year,' wrote *Observer* journalist Patrick O'Donovan.

In Spain and South American Spanish-speaking countries people tend to go home for Holy Week rather than just the Easter weekend. In Greece and Ireland Holy Week is often known as 'the Big Week'.

The purpose of Holy Week is to enable us to live with Christ his final week on earth. Through the liturgy inside and outside church we can enter Jerusalem with Christ (Palm Sunday procession), be present at the Last Supper (Maundy Thursday evening Mass), kneel in the Garden of Gethsemane (Thursday evening watch), walk with Christ as he carries the cross and then watch at the foot of the cross (procession of witness and Three Hours Service on Good Friday) and rejoice at his rising from the dead on Easter Morning (Easter Vigil). It is a week-long pilgrimage not of re-enactment but liturgical participation in Christ's suffering, death and resurrection. The celebration of the liturgy is never just the keeping of an anniversary, but an encounter, sometimes joyful, with the Lord.

'The Church relives the Passion of her Redeemer,' claimed Pope Paul VI. It is an unfolding drama which should be followed for all the eight days from glory to the depths of despair to triumph. The fourth-century Spanish nun Egeria experienced the liturgy in the Holy Land and it is her reports that helped shape the Holy Week services observed now.

In 1956 the main services were restored by the Roman Catholic Church to this basic early pattern. Ten years later they were published in English and a slight revision followed in 1971. Meanwhile the Anglican Church adopted a similar reform.

The account of Jesus' movements and actions during Holy Week is open to debate. For example the gospel writers disagree about which day Jesus overturned the tables in the Temple. Was it on his arrival on Palm Sunday when he had been given such a warm welcome or was it on Monday morning? Also, the incident with the ointment may have been, if not Saturday, next Tuesday or Wednesday night. Why was Jesus' Passover meal held a night early according to the official calendar of the day? So has the sequence been compressed from fourteen days to a week? Or was the Last Supper on Wednesday in accordance with an old calendar as claimed by Professor Colin Humphreys in his book *The Mystery of the Last Supper: Reconstructing the Final Days of Jesus*? There are differences about exactly who was first at the tomb on Easter Day. Like today's press reports of great events there are disparities and sometimes too much editing and rewriting of reports.

The most likely date for the first Holy Week is early April in AD33.

Lazarus Saturday

The Orthodox Church calls today Lazarus Saturday since Lazarus, being recently raised from the dead (see page 45), is present when Jesus arrives at Bethany. Egeria witnessed a service associated with Lazarus today at Bethany. The Orthodox glorify Christ as 'the Resurrection and the Life' who by raising Lazarus has confirmed the universal resurrection of mankind even before His own suffering and death.

What Happened Today

John 12.1-11

Jesus and the twelve disciples, walking from Jericho, arrived at Bethany to dine with the sisters Martha and Mary. Also present was their now famous brother Lazarus who, after four days in a deep tomb along the road, had been restored to life by Jesus during his last visit. This time there was a large crowd outside attracted by the preacher Jesus who had wrought the miracle.

Whilst Martha prepared the meal, Mary suddenly produced some expensive perfume and anointed Jesus' feet which had probably just been washed after the long journey. At once Judas Iscariot gives the first clue of his hostility to the master by asking if the ointment should not have been sold and given to the poor.

Jesus reply is that they will always have the poor with them but that he will not always be physically with them. This may also have been a hint that Mary was anointing his body ready for his coming death.

The site of the house in Bethany where Jesus stayed is occupied by the Church of St Lazarus, built only in the 1950s and run by Franciscans. A few yards up the road is Lazarus' empty tomb. Sometime during his five-night stay Jesus also spent time at the home of Simon where both Matthew and Mark suggest that the ointment incident may have taken place on another night.

Bethany is part of a town called al-Eizariya.

In Church

At Mass this morning the gospel reading (John 11.45-56) is the account of high priest Caiaphas and the Pharisees, an orthodox Jewish sect, expressing concern about Jesus' popularity following his last visit to Bethany. Caiaphas hints at what is to come by observing that it is better for one man to die...'.

Evensong and Vespers look to Palm Sunday tomorrow.

Palm Sunday

Today is the first day of Holy Week when the main Mass is preceded by the outdoor palm procession recalling Christ riding into Jerusalem.

What Happened Today
Matthew 21.1-11; Mark 11.1-11; Luke 19.28-44; John 12.12-19

In the morning Jesus, who had spent the night with his disciples at Bethany, asked two of them to go to nearby Bethphage and bring the donkey and colt tethered there. He added that if anyone asked what they were doing they were to say: 'The Master needs them and will send them back at once.'

Kings would normally arrive by horse but Jesus rode on a donkey when he set out for Jerusalem. The twelve main disciples laid their cloaks on the donkey for a saddle and as Jesus mounted, other supporters, attracted by news of Jesus's miracles and teaching, spread their own cloaks on the ground. They also laid and waved newly cut palm branches which were a national symbol of Judaea brandished at times of celebration and depicted on coins.

Matthew and John, recording the event, recall words in the Book of the Prophet Zechariah (9.9): 'Look, your king is approaching ... humble and riding on a donkey'. They see the rider as the universal king of peace and of the poor.

The two-mile route was to the top of the Mount of Olives, for the first view of Jerusalem, and then down the rough road behind the Garden of Gethsemane into the Kedron Valley.

Here on the downward slope the crowd shouted: 'Hosanna

to the Son of David!', 'Blessed is he who is coming in the name of the Lord!' and 'Hosanna in the highest heavens!' The phrases reflect psalm 118 sung in procession at Jewish festivals.

Some Pharisees asked Jesus to stop these chants but he replied, with reference to the rocks on the hillside, that if they kept silent 'the stones will cry out'.

Ahead, up the final slope was the Golden Gate leading directly to the Temple area in the walled city of Jerusalem. People, who had heard about the miracles including Lazarus being brought back to life, came out of the city to greet the procession. Christ was acknowledged by the crowd as 'the prophet Jesus from Nazareth in Galilee'. This worried the Pharisees who feared that Jesus had almost total support.

In the evening Jesus and his party returned to Bethany. This road remained rough until the middle of the twentieth century and the gate still exists although it is now sealed as part of the long city wall.

Procession

The church procession represents Jesus' donkey ride from Bethany to Jerusalem. The route should begin outside the church and even at another building such as the hall, school or pub forecourt.

Donkeys sometimes feature in the processions and in view of the mention in Matthew of a donkey and a colt it is not inappropriate to have two donkeys.

The vestments for the procession are red for the royalty of Christ the King.

The congregation, by joining in the outdoor procession led by the clergy, publicly professes its loyalty to Christ. The procession, from starting point to church door, is the journey from Bethany to Jerusalem. The church is Jerusalem where this week the Last Supper, the crucifixion and resurrection will be recalled. Today is a pointer to the glory of Easter although there is much to experience first.

Anyone waiting at the church door for the procession can

liken themselves to those who came out of Jerusalem to welcome Christ. Members of the congregation are not mere spectators but a vital part of the liturgy.

The earliest record of a Palm Sunday procession is about three hundred and ninety in Jerusalem when at around 5pm there was a huge procession from the Mount of Olives with everyone carrying palms and olive branches and chanting Psalm 118 and 'Blessed is he who comes in the name of the Lord'. Before setting out the gospel account was read aloud. All this was witnessed by the Spanish nun Egeria (see page 52). By the next century Spain was the first western country to have a Palm Sunday procession. Today the procession in Jerusalem along the actual route still takes place in the afternoon (see below).

In Saxon times the outdoor palm procession at Canterbury Cathedral began at St Martin's Church, appropriately on a hill looking down on the city. Here after 1070 Archbishop Lanfranc introduced the custom of carrying the host in the procession so that Christ was present as on the first Palm Sunday. This became a feature of the English palm procession with Chichester Cathedral and St Albans Abbey having special vessels for the sacrament on this annual occasion. In Germany and Poland there was often a life-size wooden figure of Christ on a donkey pulled on wheels. St Kolumba's in Cologne used one until 1778.

Palm crosses are distributed before setting out this morning. Sometimes indigenous palms are used. In England five hundred years ago it would have been box, willow and yew. In Kent the yew tree was known as the palm. During World War II myrtle was used. Even in the years after the Reformation, when there were few processions, it was the custom for people to wear a spray of willow today and churches continued to be decorated with willow and catkins which are still often used today.

In Austria and Poland, the palms or catkin twigs are often decorated with bright ribbons or flowers. Olive branches are used in Italy. Today's dried palm leaves come from Tanzania, usually folded into the shape of a cross, or Elche near Valencia in southern Spain where the palm groves were planted by the

Moors. In February two refrigerated containers from Spain arrive at Liverpool full of palm leaves for Hayes and Finch where temporary staff strip, bundle and pack them. Clergy often carry long dried branches which can be used over several years.

The palms are blessed and sprinkled with holy water before an account of the first Palm Sunday is read from one of the gospels.

Hymns sung during the procession usually include *All glory, laud and honour*, written by St Theodulph Bishop of Orleans in 818 for the procession in Angers. The original version *Gloria, Laus et Honor* ran to thirty-nine verses but today's six-verse hymn is the result of a translation in 1851 by J. M. Neale.

In Church

The congregation may enter church in procession singing Psalm 23 which was sung by Jews entering the Temple. The responsorial psalm later in the Roman Catholic Mass is Christ's words on the cross taken from Psalm 2, 'My God, my God, why have you forsaken me?' The long story of Christ's last two days before death in one of the gospels is sometimes sung by at least three voices with the congregation invited to join in calling out the crowd's words. The hymn *My song is love unknown* has an apt verse for today.

Vestments are red as in the procession.

Palm Sunday Processions and Custom

Jerusalem

In Jerusalem, today's big procession is at 2.30pm along the original route beginning at Bethphage Church which has a mounting stone said to have been used by Christ. The procession enters Old Jerusalem by St Stephen's Gate, which replaces the Temple's now closed Golden Gate, used on the first occasion. Many people carry fresh green palms which give a more authentic feel than the dried version used in church. Participants include Scout bands, local congregations, clergy, pilgrims and the Latin Patriarch of Jerusalem. The procession concludes with a ceremony in the courtyard of Saint Anne's Church just inside the gate. More than 10,000 people took part in 1980 but, after a drop to around 3000 caused by recent unrest, numbers are now about 15,000. George Carey took part in 2002 during his last year as Archbishop of Canterbury.

Vatican

In Rome the Pope goes to the St Peter's Square obelisk to bless palms in the form of olive branches, dried palms and large fresh palm branches. Some come from Elche and Puglia. But since 1586 most of the palms have come from Bordighera or neighbouring Sanremo on the Italian Riviera which became famous for palms thanks to St Ampelio who in 411 brought the stones of date palms from Egypt. It is claimed that a Bordigheran sailor was in Rome when the obelisk in St Peter's Square was being erected and prevented disaster by loudly calling for the taught ropes to be soaked in water to stop them from snapping. The obelisk was originally brought to Rome from Heliopolis by the Roman Emperor Caligula.

The procession makes its way to the steps of St Peter's basilica for the open-air Mass. Since 1984, after John Paul II claimed that it was young people who welcomed Christ to Jerusalem on the first Palm Sunday, this has also been World Youth Day. Around three hundred young people from many nations take part in the procession representing the rest of the vast congregation who for logistical reasons cannot join in.

Spain

In Elche, which has produced palm branches since 1492, there is naturally a huge and impressive palm procession to the Basilica of Santa Maria on Sunday morning, with some of the white palms turned into clever decorations and many families joining in carrying tall palm branches. The highlight is the figure of Christ on a donkey in a sea of palms carried shoulder-high.

New York, USA
The congregation of Trinity Church Wall Street gathers at St Paul's Chapel and makes its way down Broadway to Trinity.

England
Many parishes and cathedrals are increasingly returning to holding the pre-procession gathering and liturgy in a prominent public location away from the church. This is both an act of mission as well as a visible recall of the entry into Jerusalem.

Winchester Cathedral's procession with a donkey starts half a mile away in the castle's Great Hall to pass into the city at the West Gate as it did as early as 1110. At Lincoln the procession from the castle passes through the cathedral's covered Exchequer gate. At Hereford Cathedral the route retains some of the elements of the medieval Palm Sunday with a stop outside the cathedral's west front where from a gallery choristers sing the same chant as their pre-Reformation predecessors.

London's Borough Market is the gathering point for the congregation of Southwark Cathedral. St Mary's, Primrose Hill starts on top of Parliament Hill. The York Minister procession has started outside Bettys Tea Rooms whilst St Mark's Wimbledon begins at Tesco.

The St Martin-in-the-Fields congregation meets at Admiralty Arch to walk across Trafalgar Square led by a donkey who mounts the church steps before being led down the central aisle and out the vestry door. At Gloucester Cathedral a chorister rides a donkey down the nave as part of the procession from St Mary de Lode Church.

Since 2008 St Paul's Cathedral has maintained a procession with two donkeys starting in Paternoster Square and passing under the Temple Bar gateway to represent Jerusalem's gate.

At Silchester in Hampshire an ecumenical palm procession sets off at 10am from the village and passes through the site of the Roman town. One of the stops made is near the outline of the church that is the earliest known place of Christian worship in the Winchester Diocese. In addition to the carrying of palms by participants there is a donkey, and men dressed as Roman soldiers. The procession arrives at the Roman amphitheatre near the present isolated church in time for an open-air Anglican Eucharist. This custom began in 1984.

For St Christopher's in Liverpool's Norris Green it is the large porch of the Co-op supermarket at the opposite end of Broad Lane which is Bethany.

Hentland Pax Cake Custom

In about 1570 the will of Lady Scudamore, who wished to encourage peace and good fellowship, provided for her estate to give five shillings a year for slices of cake and ale for the parishioners of Hentland, Selleck and King's Capel in Herefordshire. By the middle of the nineteenth century, ale had disappeared but small cakes were still offered from baskets, covered with white cloths, just after the collection had been taken during the Palm Sunday service. Now the church pays for a pax cake to be given out to everyone attending from the parish of Hentland-with-Hoarwithy. The inedible hard flat 'cakes', made in Ross-on-Wye, are stamped with the Pascal Lamb. As each person leaves Hentland Church after Palm Sunday evensong they are handed a cake by the incumbent who says: 'God and good neighbourhood.' The setting for the ceremony was for many years the late nineteenth-century Italianate daughter church at Hoarwithy, described by Sir Roy Strong as 'a little bit of Sicily', where in 1980 few attended on Palm Sunday afternoon. Numbers have recently increased with the custom returning to the mother church.

Monday of Holy Week
Fig Monday

Today is sometimes called Fig Monday, just as until the end of the nineteenth century Palm Sunday was often known as Fig Sunday in the Midlands, Cotswolds and parts of Yorkshire and Wiltshire. Flora Thompson mentions eating figs in *Lark Rise to Candleford*. Figs and figgy pudding were eaten in remembrance of the fig tree noted by Christ on the Bethany-Jerusalem road (Matthew 21.18-19; Mark 11.12-14). *Bethany* means *house of the figs* and *Bethphage*, where the donkeys were tethered, is *house of early figs*. Jesus mentions the tree in his talk to the disciples on the Mount of Olives later this week (see page 64). Although fresh figs were not in season, fig cakes would have been eaten at the Last Supper on Maundy Thursday (see page 70).

What Happened Today
Matthew 21.12-16; Mark 11.15-19; Luke 19.45-46; John

This morning Jesus sets out again from Bethany but this time just with the twelve followers. On the way he looks at a fig tree but it has no fruit since it is too early in the summer. 'May no one ever eat fruit from you again', is his surprising comment.

On arriving at the Temple area he picked up a cord and began driving out those who were there trading at stalls. He upset the rival bureau de change tables and those selling pigeons and sheep for sacrifice.

Then he began teaching the onlookers who were mostly visitors to Jerusalem for the coming Passover. He reminded them of words in Isaiah 56.7, 'My house will be called a house of prayer for all peoples'. Traders being removed from the Temple had been foretold in Zechariah 14.21.

Jesus, probably referring to the sale of doves for sacrifice at a massively inflated price, accused the traders of turning the Temple into 'a bandits' den' as suggested in Jeremiah 7.11.

Children watching all the activity took up yesterday's cry of 'Hosanna to the Son of David'. In the First Book of Maccabees it is recorded that palm branches were carried to celebrate the purification and cleansing of the Temple in 167BC and 141BC so it is significant that palms featured in Jesus' procession on the eve of his own Temple cleansing. He declined to silence the children who were caught up in their parents' excitement.

In the evening Jesus went back to Bethany leaving the chief priests concerned at the attention he was continuing to command.

In Church
The vestments continue to be red until Thursday.

Sacrament of Reconciliation
Early this week is the time when many make their confession so as to be absolved from their sins before Easter weekend. This is to give a fresh start and a new beginning ready for the Easter season. Clergy are always available to hear confessions but an increasing number of churches have a reconciliation service this evening, or tomorrow. Tuesday, when there is time for preparation and a long prayerful interval when members of the congregation can go and make their individual confession privately.

Tuesday of Holy Week

What Happened Today

Matthew 26.1-13; Mark 11.20-13.37; Luke 19.47-21.38;
John 12.20

On the way in to Jerusalem for the third time Jesus and his companions pass the fig tree which appeared to have withered. In the city he spends the day teaching in the Temple where the wary chief priests asked him, without direct success, by what authority he acted and spoke. But he did attempt speaking to them in parables. The parable of the tenant farmers was an attack on the Jewish authorities which they recognised although they failed to heed the warning about killing the son.

At this time he dealt with the trick question from the Pharisees who asked whether they should pay taxes to Caesar. Holding up a coin he said: 'Pay Caesar what belongs to Caesar – and God what belongs to God.' This is the quotation used today by Christians when they have to disobey a law which goes against Christian teaching. Such situations arose in Nazi Germany and communist states.

He also pointed out the old lady putting two small value coins in the collecting box saying: 'This poor widow has put more in than all who have contributed to the treasury; for they have all put in money they could spare, but she in her poverty has put in everything she possessed, all she had to live on.'

Amongst visitors to the Temple were some Greeks who asked to meet Jesus. This both harks back to the visit of the Three Kings of several nations in Bethlehem and represents the mission of the church which will involve many nationalities.

Later, when Jesus was sitting on the Mount of Olives with

Peter, James, John and Andrew, he was asked what was going to happen. Jesus began a long discourse and mentioned the fig tree which they passed every day on the Bethany road. This may have been a reference to those who would not hear and the fate of the Temple. He likened a bud indicating the approach of summer to the signs hinting that the Kingdom of God was near.

In the evening the party almost certainly returned to Bethany as Matthew suggests that the incident with the ointment (see page 53) took place at tonight's meal rather than last Saturday. But Luke appears to hint that Jesus may have stayed on the Mount of Olives and slept outside.

In Church

The vestments are red.

Wednesday of Holy Week
Spy Wednesday

It is mainly in Ireland that today is known as Spy Wednesday. This is a reminder that today Judas Iscariot secretly agreed to become a spy for the Sanhedrin, the supreme Jewish council that acted as a civil court for Jerusalem. Judas' decision led to the arrest of Christ late on Thursday night.

When Egeria, the Spanish nun, was in the Holy Land about 390 she heard read aloud today the story of Judas going to betray Christ. At the end, she reported, the congregation audibly 'moaned and groaned'.

What Happened Today
Mark 14.1-11; Matthew 26.14-16

We can assume from the four gospel accounts that Jesus spent today, as the last two days, teaching in the Temple although some suggest that he rested at Bethany.

Judas Iscariot, one of Christ's twelve followers, was able to be in Jerusalem where he approached the chief priests and elders of the Temple offering to assist in Jesus' arrest. They wanted to find him when he was alone and far away from the adoring crowds. Judas enquired how much he could be paid for his assistance. It appears that he may have been given the thirty pieces of silver in advance.

The coins were either the Jewish silver shekel or the Roman silver denarius, worth a considerable sum because later they were used to buy a field. But Matthew, who records an actual amount, may have been relying on Zechariah 11.13 for the figure.

Why Judas did this is unclear although John suggests that Judas was the group treasurer and used to help himself from the common fund (John 12.6). Judas also criticised Mary for pouring expensive ointment on Jesus (see Eve of Palm Sunday, page 53). As the only non-Galilean he may have felt himself to be an outsider despite Christ reaching out even in recent days to others.

In the evening Jesus was as usual in Bethany and probably dining at the home of Simon. Maybe the villagers had shared out the task of feeding and finding beds for Jesus and his twelve followers. Lazarus was present and Martha cooked the meal.

In Church

The psalm at Mass today hints at what is to come on Good Friday with reference to 'taunts'. The Roman Catholic gospel reading (Matthew 26.14-25) is an account of the betrayal of Jesus by Judas Iscariot as heard by Egeria.

There is no reserved sacrament left in the tabernacle after today's Mass as tomorrow evening the church celebrates the institution of the Eucharist when everyone present will receive Holy Communion consecrated that night in their presence.

Some churches sing *Tenebrae* this evening.

Tenebrae

The name *Tenebrae* comes from the Latin word for *darkness* or *shadows* and is first mentioned in the early twelfth century by Peter Abelard. It is a combination of monastic matins and lauds for Maundy Thursday sung tonight in anticipation.

In monastic houses these services would normally have been sung in the darkness of the very early hours. Over the three nights of Spy Wednesday, Maundy Thursday and Good Friday they were combined and often sung much earlier so that the laity could attend. In the nineteenth century the Pope attended *Tenebrae* of Thursday sung as early as 4pm today.

The focus of the two-hour service is a triangular candle stand known as a hearse which is placed before the altar. *Hearse* is corruption of *harrow* suggested by the spikes for the candles. There are normally fifteen candles – seven on each sloping side representing Mary Magdalene, Mary wife of Cleophas (see page 100) and the twelve Apostles whilst on top there is a white candle for Christ. In the past the number of lights varied with the Sarum Rite prescribing twenty-four whilst Coutances Cathedral in Normandy had as many as forty-four. The candles, which can be unbleached as at a funeral, are extinguished one by one as each psalm is finished recalling a deepening gloom as Christ is abandoned by his followers.

Near the beginning is the singing of the Lamentations in the form of three lessons from the Old Testament's First Lamentation of Jeremiah (Lamentations 1:1-14). The sad haunting chant forms part of the Jewish liturgy which would have been heard by Christ. Appropriately, being Spy Wednesday, tonight's *Tenebrae* has many graphic references to Judas Iscariot.

Near the end of the service there is the Song of Moses which will be heard again on Saturday after the Easter Vigil's third reading.

During the Benedictus the other candles in church are put out leaving only the white candle at the top of the triangle burning. This light is then hidden behind the altar whilst Psalm 51, usually Allegri's Miserere (see page 86), is sung.

Soon after a loud noise is made off-stage like a clap of thunder. This is the Strepitus, or Great Noise, said to represent confusion, the crowd seeking Christ' arrest at Gethsemane or an earthquake at Christ's death or resurrection. It has been suggested that the noise is merely a development of the abbot knocking on a bench top to indicate that the service is over. However, it is not over as the hidden light is brought back to the pinnacle of the triangle. This represents Christ overcoming death on Easter morning.

'This arduous service has mystical beauty,' observed art historian Brian Sewell who described it as 'the most disturbing and convincing service', which was also 'poetic, theatrical and terrible'. The responses are sometimes described as 'ethereal'.

Until 1956, when Holy Week Services were updated, many would have been familiar with Tenebrae sung in the early evening at Westminster Cathedral and Brompton Oratory. Then for a few years *Tenebrae* was restored to the morning where it belonged. But in 1972 the office of *Tenebrae* was abolished although not proscribed. The Oratory continues to sing Tenebrae on Good Friday and Holy Saturday morning without the Miserere, a hiding of the light or a clap of thunder. The Dominicans at Blackfriars Oxford also sing *Tenebrae* but, in their tradition, neither hide the light nor make a noise. Today it is sung at 4pm in the Holy Sepulchre in Jerusalem.

London churches with a strong musical tradition which sing *Tenebrae* tonight as an introduction to the Triduum (see page 76) include All Saints Margaret Street, St Paul's Covent Garden and St Mary Moorfields. In 2017 St John's Smith Square, although now a concert venue, first staged the singing of *Tenebrae* by candlelight at 10pm with plans to make it an annual event at 3am the next morning to coincide with the original hour.

Tenebrae starts in blazing light and ends in darkness with a single light. The Easter Vigil (see page 92) will start in darkness with a single light and end in a blaze of light.

The Book of Occasional Services used by Episcopalians (Anglicans) in the USA has provision for *Tenebrae* which can be heard tonight at Trinity Wall Street in New York and St Ann Chapel in Palo Alto, California.

Maundy Thursday
Holy Thursday in Ireland

The word *Maundy* comes from the Latin word *mandatum* meaning *commandment* found in the gospel acclamation (antiphon) for today *Mandatum novum de vobis* (*I give you a new commandment: love one another just as I have loved you*) from St John's Gospel 13.34. On the first Maundy Thursday Christ commanded followers 'to love one another' and washed his followers' feet.

This morning most cathedrals have a Chrism Mass and in one the Queen distributes the Royal Maundy. However, the main church service today is this evening's Mass of Lord's Supper which is followed by the Gethsemane watch to midnight.

The Last Supper is recognised as the institution of Holy Communion. Bread and wine become sacramentally the body and blood of Christ when prayed over by those given authority handed down from Christ. Roman Catholics and catholic Anglicans believe that Christ is present under the appearance of bread and wine at the celebration of the Eucharist.

In the Holy Communion at the Lord's Supper we are all reconciled with Jesus as he asked. By the gift of the Eucharist he called on the disciples to share his mission.

Today is a public holiday in Denmark, Spain and Norway. Until 2007 today in the UK remained a non-working day for electoral purposes meaning that Maundy Thursday could not be election day.

What Happened Today
Matthew 26.17-75; Mark 14.12-72; Luke 22.7-65; John 13.1-18.27

Preparation for a Meal

Today the disciples asked Jesus where they should prepare their Passover meal to be eaten tonight. He sent Peter and John into Jerusalem and told them to follow a man carrying a pitcher of water to a house. They were to ask him to show them the dining room. Christ assured them that they would be shown an upstairs room where they could make preparations. It was not unusual for families to hire a room for Passover in Jerusalem.

The Last Supper

It is called the Last Supper because it was the last time that Christ and his disciples ate together. These disciples were the twelve closest to Jesus.

All went according to Jesus' plan and in the evening, probably after 6pm, he arrived at the chosen house and went up to the room furnished with couches. Jesus and some of his followers had been dining together all week in Bethany but tonight he was possibly alone with his twelve inner group of disciples. This meal may not have been a normal Passover meal. It was a day early, unless Jesus was observing an alternative ancient calendar, and a Passover meal would always include women and children. His mother Mary, who was in Jerusalem, would have been a natural guest if this was a Passover meal. Passover commemorates the deliverance of the Children of Israel from slavery and so the meal features unleavened bread, sometimes called matzah or matzo, to recall bread baked hurriedly when the Jewish people fled Egypt. It is a meal full of symbolism which includes laying a place for Elijah who heralds the coming of the Messiah.

First Jesus removed a garment and wrapped a towel round his waist to wash the feet of the disciples (John 13.4-15). Peter was overwhelmed at this act, usually undertaken by servants or humble people, and tried to resist but Jesus insisted. 'If I, then, your Lord and Master, have washed your feet, you should wash each other's feet. I have given you an example so that you may copy what I have done to you.' Knowing there was a dispute, about which of them was the greatest, Jesus warned that any leader must behave as if he was the one who serves.

During the first course Jesus warned that one of them would betray him. The shocked disciples, including Judas, said: 'Not me, Lord, surely?' But when John, sitting next to Christ, asked who it was, Jesus replied that it was the disciple 'to whom I shall give the bread that I dip in the dish'. As soon as Judas had accepted the bread he left. The others were still puzzled and may have believed that he had gone to buy something.

It was usual for the head of the household to distribute pieces of the flat bread before the Pascal lamb was eaten. But now Jesus broke a piece of the bread, blessed it and said: 'This is my body.' He then picked up a cup of wine saying: 'This is my blood.' The episode is the institution of the Eucharist and the first Holy Communion (Matthew 26.26-28; Mark 14.22-25; Luke 22.17-20). St Paul later wrote of the importance of coming together for the Lord's Supper (I Corinthians 11.23-26).

By about 8pm Jesus spoke at some length giving what was his farewell discourse to the future leaders of the Church. It was a message of reassurance and he gave a hint of the Trinity saying that he would send the Holy Spirit. The latter came at Pentecost (page 139) and the former we celebrate on Trinity Sunday (page 153). So the eleven disciples left at the table, instructed to offer bread and wine in remembrance, became the Apostles, or first bishops, and all priests are the assistants of their successors.

Tonight Jesus founded the Church by appealing to his followers to remain united and it is this call which is remembered every year during the Week of Prayer for Christian Unity in January..

Gethsemane

At the end of the meal they sang psalms 113 to 118, as is traditional at the end of a Passover meal, before setting out downhill on a walk of about twenty minutes to the Garden of Gethsemane across the valley at the foot of the Mount of Olives. It would now be at least approaching 10pm. Jesus may have given the impression to others that he was setting off back to Bethany as usual or maybe to sleep on the Mount of Olives.

But tonight he was to get no further than Gethsemane at the foot of the hill where he stopped to pray and urged others to keep awake.

At around midnight Judas appeared and greeted Jesus with a customary kiss. The chief priests finding Jesus alone in the dark garden decided to arrest him earlier than maybe intended.

Detention at Caiaphas' House
Jesus was taken across the Kidron Valley and up a long flight of steps to the house of the chief priest, Caiaphas. After appearing before the high priests, Jesus was detained for what little remained of the night.

The site of Caiaphas' house is now St Peter in Gallicantu, the Cockcrow Church. Peter, who had followed at a distance, denied knowing Jesus and as he heard a cock at 6am he remembered Jesus' words: 'Before the cock crows twice, you will have disowned me three times.'

Relics

Valencia Cathedral in Spain displays a 3.5 inches diameter dark red agate cup known as the Santo Caliz and said to be the one used by Christ at the Last Supper. Both Pope John Paul II and Benedict XVI visited Valencia and celebrated Mass using the cup. Italy's Genoa Cathedral also holds a dish which was for centuries said to be the Holy Grail but is now thought to date to medieval times. Spain's Coria Cathedral keeps, in its chapel of relics, a cup and a table cloth claimed as having been used during the Last Supper. Leon Cathedral in Spain has, embedded in a medieval chalice, an onyx cup dating from the Roman period which in 2014 historians Margarita Torres and José Ortega del Río strongly claimed to be the original. A Vatican Museum curator once suggested that the cup used by Christ was probably glass.

In a Cathedral Today: Chrism Mass

In the morning clergy from parishes and elsewhere gather in their cathedral for a Mass during which the bishop blesses the oils. Today is the day when Christ not only gave the Church the gift of the Eucharist but also instituted the priesthood and so, at the instigation of Pope Paul VI, the clergy renew their ordination vows. It was also the Pope's idea for all clergy to concelebrate at this Mass with their bishop.

The tradition of blessing the oils on Maundy Thursday morning goes back to the fifth century. But the gathering of clergy for this special Mass dates only from 1956 when the Maundy Thursday Mass of the Lord's Supper in parishes was moved from 9am in the morning to the evening.

Olive oil was seen by Jews as a sign of God's favour and it is also the lifeblood of society. The Queen was anointed with oil at her coronation.

James, brother of Jesus and church leader in Jerusalem, wrote that if a person was sick then a priest must be called to 'anoint the sick person with oil in the name of the Lord and pray over him' (James 5.14).

The Oil of the Sick (for use in ministry of sick and dying), the Oil of Catachumens (for those being baptised) and the Oil of Chrism (for use at confirmations, ordinations and consecrations) which gives its name to this Mass, are all blessed. The latter is a mixture of olive oil to which the bishop adds balsam (aromatic vegetable oils) before breathing on the vessel's opening to signify the Holy Spirit coming down to sanctify it.

Laity are asked to be present to support their clergy. In 1999 Cardinal Hume said that the occasion would not be complete without the presence of lay people who are served by the clergy. As soon as the priests have renewed their ordination vows, the bishop addresses the people asking for them to pray for their clergy and for him.

The hymn *Redeemer, Lord, your praise we sing* was written by Michael Saward for the Chrism Eucharist at St Paul's Cathedral.

This can be a long service but even if it is completed with dignity in seventy-five minutes it might still take ten minutes for the procession of diocesan clergy to leave the cathedral. Afterwards clergy collect oil for use in the parish during the coming year. Today the church begins to renew itself for Easter and the rest of the year.

Increasingly cathedrals are holding the Chrism Mass earlier in the week so that clergy do not have to travel a long distance today.

Royal Maundy Service

This morning the Queen, accompanied by her Chapel Royal and the Yeoman of the Guard, goes to a cathedral or collegiate church to present Maundy money. This public act, which helps to keep the day special in people's minds, can be traced back to King John who, at Knaresborough Castle on Maundy Thursday 1210, followed Christ's example at the Last Supper by washing the feet of some poor men. The king also gave them a girdle, a knife and breeches and then fed a thousand people. Three years later at Rochester Cathedral he also gave money which later became the main feature of today's annual ceremony. In 1363 Edward III washed the feet of as many poor as his age. At this time those chosen still had to be of the same sex as the monarch.

At Greenwich in 1572 the ceremonial involved feet being washed four times: first by the laundress (using a silver basin filled with warm water and sweet flowers), then, after a hymn, by the Sub-Almoner and Lord High Almoner. Only after the reading of John 13:1-16 did Elizabeth I enter to wash and kiss the feet in person. Elizabeth began the regular money present, in the form of silver pennies, which was in addition to gifts of cloth, herrings, wine and bread.

In 1667 Charles II left the washing to the Bishop of London but in 1670 introduced the specially minted and dated coins. The last sovereign to wash feet was James II in 1685 when the Chapel Royal Register records the king having 'wash'd, wip'd, and kiss'd the feet of 52 poor men with wonderful humility'. He was also the last monarch to be present and in the following years it was undertaken on the sovereign's behalf with the last foot washing, by the Archbishop of York as the Lord High Almoner, being in 1736. Under George I recipients included women.

At this time until 1890 the ceremony was in the Whitehall Banqueting House which had become a chapel. In the 1750s this took place at 4pm.

In 1931 Princess Helena Victoria, having carried out the distribution in Westminster Abbey, suggested to the Secretary to the Royal Almonry that George V ought to attend and if invited to do so he might agree. He did and became the first monarch since James II to attend the ceremony. Nosegays of sweet herbs and flowers, originally to ward off the smell of feet, are carried in the procession. The Lord High Almoner, a diocesan bishop, opens the service by reading the account of Jesus washing the disciples' feet and then, although there is no longer foot washing, removes his cope and mitre to wear a linen towel over his alb whilst accompanying the Queen at the distribution of purses. Royal Almonry officials wear towels dating from 1883. Four local children girded in towels and holding posies become for the day Children of the Royal Almonry representing those once helped with foot washing.

Her Majesty has introduced a policy of giving the purses to local retired people aged over 70 involved in working for the community. From Henry IV's reign in the early fifteenth century the total number related to the age of the monarch but since the eighteenth century the number of both male and female recipients has matched the age of the monarch. Two soft leather purses are given out together. (Until 1979 the Queen did a separate distribution of a third purse with the clothing money.) A white one contains the same number of pence as the Queen's age on her next birthday in specially minted silver pennies, twopences, threepences and fourpences. (Gold coins were minted in Coronation Year 1953.) A red purse contains £5.50 in normal cash representing £3 for clothing, £1.50 for provisions and £1 for the redemption of the Queen's gown. In 2005 this was given in the form of a £5 coin commemorating the Trafalgar Victory and a 50p piece celebrating the creation of Dr Johnson's Dictionary of 1755. In 2006 the £5 payment was made with the Queen's 80th birthday coin.

The Yeomen of the Guard carry the purses on giant dishes but the custom of bearing them on their heads was discontinued as the weight increased with so many purses due to the Queen's great age.

In Church Tonight
The Triduum Part 1

This evening sees the start of the Triduum which is one service in three sections with long gaps over three days. Triduum comes from the Latin *Sacrum Triduum* meaning *Sacred Three*. The three are tonight's Evening Mass, tomorrow afternoon's Good Friday liturgy and Saturday evening's Easter Vigil. 'The Easter Triduum is the apex of our liturgical year and it is also the apex of our lives as Christians', observed Pope Francis.

Evening Mass of the Lord's Supper

Today is partly a joyful occasion as it marks the institution of the Eucharist. But as we know that on the same day Christ was arrested so the full celebration and thanksgiving for the Eucharist must wait until Corpus Christi (see page 157). The Anglican post-Communion prayer is the Corpus Christi collect.

Tonight's service has a beginning but no formal end for it is just the first part of a single Easter Triduum liturgy which will only be completed with the Easter Vigil.

The entrance or offertory procession can include the parish's own allocation of oils blessed in the cathedral this morning (see page 72).

Bells are rung at beginning of the Gloria but not as vigorously as they will be when it is sung again at the Easter Vigil.

The first reading is about the Jews' deliverance from slavery (Exodus 12.1-14) which gave rise to the Passover meal. The second reading, from St Paul's letter to the Corinthians, is the oldest written account of the Lord's Supper.

The feet of twelve people are washed although it need not be as many as twelve.

This is not a reenactment and so in 2016 Pope Francis made

it clear that the 'group may consist of men and women, and ideally of the young and the old'. Earlier increasingly ignored guidance had confined the number to men.

Like Christ, the priest removes an outer garment (the chasuble) and wraps a towel round the waist to be ready to wash feet. This usually takes the form of pouring water over a right foot and drying it with a towel. Foot washing was introduced in 1955. Prior to this any foot-washing ceremonies had been separate occasions.

After the Communion there is the transfer of the Blessed Sacrament in the form of the bread to a side chapel representing Christ and his fellow diners walking to the Garden of Gethsemane. During the procession there is usually the singing of the Corpus Christi hymn *Of the glorious body telling* (Pange Lingua; see page 163). The last two verses (*Tantum ergo*) are sung when the chapel has been reached. Tonight's procession is a sombre version of the outdoor Corpus Christi procession and in some churches the congregation is invited to join in this Maundy Thursday procession (maybe carrying candles) and so follow Christ, in the Blessed Sacrament, through the night to Gethsemane.

Other suitable hymns include *Sweet sacrament divine* and *Ubi Caritas*.

The church is made bare, stripped of cloths, cushions, books and candles, to represent Christ being abandoned by friends and stripped on Good Friday. Meanwhile the choir may sing Psalm 22 which opens with words spoken tomorrow from memory by Christ on the cross, 'My God, my God, why have you forsaken me?' and includes a foretelling of his guards' actions with the words 'they divide my garments among them; they cast lots for my clothing'.

There is no dismissal. The vigil in Gethsemane has already begun and the congregation is invited to be there too with Christ.

Watch
The chapel where the consecrated bread has been taken represents the Garden of Gethsemane. Flowering plants in pots and flowers

around the altar are both in honour of the Blessed Sacrament and a reminder of the garden. The many candles maintain the sense of a dark garden. The watch, or vigil, should not last beyond midnight. Obviously it is difficult for many to be present for the whole evening. Indeed one must eat just as the disciples had before they went to the garden. Since Christ asked his very tired followers to stay awake to watch and pray for just one hour it is reasonable to attempt at least an hour.

At midnight the sacrament can be removed and the candles put out. The end of the vigil marks the moment of Christ's arrest about this time. At Southwark Cathedral the end is signalled when the silence is broken with the words from the Matthew (26.45) account: 'The hour has come when the Son of man is to be betrayed into the hands of sinners.'

It is the custom in Rome, as in some other European capitals, for families to pay a brief visit to vigils in different churches to compare decorations. The Roman custom of visiting seven churches tonight may be derived from a pilgrim tradition of calling in on the Seven Pilgrim Churches of Rome.

Today in Jerusalem

The Latin Patriarch and the Orthodox Patriarch hold foot-washing ceremonies this morning in the Holy Sepulchre Church. The Franciscan Custos presides at another in the Cenacle, the building occupying the site of the Upper Room where the Last Supper was held.

In the afternoon many people visit the Cenacle. At the Garden of Gethsemane basilica there is the Mass of the Last Supper at 5pm. Afterwards groups from nearby churches visit following their own services and at 9pm there is a Holy Hour in several languages. The Church of St Peter in Gallicantu, site of Jesus night-time imprisonment, remains open most of the night.

Good Friday

Good Friday comes from *God's Friday*. Abroad it can be called Holy or Great Friday. In Scandinavia it is Long Friday. Germany calls it Silent Friday.

Today has been observed since the fourth century as a separate occasion from Easter which is yet to come.

Today was an accepted day off from work long before the 1871 Bank Holidays Act. Good Friday, like Christmas Day, remains a common law holiday in England and Wales. In Ireland the pubs remain closed. In Scotland today has been a Bank Holiday since 1871. Cuba restored the holiday in 2012.

The church services are inevitably long and not suitable for noisy babies or young children. In London some families find the centuries old 'Hot Cross Bun service' at St Bartholomew's to be an ideal introduction to Good Friday worship (see below). Many towns hold ecumenical processions of witness which can involve children.

Fast Day

Today, like Ash Wednesday, is a day of fasting and abstinence. Services starting during lunchtime make the fasting and abstinence easier to achieve than maybe at the start of Lent. Traditionally the day in England often begins with hot cross buns for breakfast.

What Happened Today

Matthew 27.1-61; Mark 15.1-14; Luke 23.1-56; John 8.29-9.42
Jesus was put to death because he upset both the Temple authorities and the Romans. Following his arrest on Thursday, Jesus had no sleep. At first light he appeared before the Sanhedrin, the supreme Jewish court, which had his hands bound before handing him to Roman governor Pontius Pilate.

He sent him to Herod who swiftly returned Jesus to the governor who asked Jesus: 'Are you the king of the Jews?' Jesus just said: 'It is you who say it.' The chief priests made many accusations but Jesus said nothing more.

Being the Passover, it was usual for the governor to release one prisoner and Pilate suggested that it should be Jesus. However, the crowd watching the exchanges and egged on by the chief priests, called out the name of Barabbas who was also being held.

'What am I to do with Jesus who is called Christ?' asked Pilate and in reply the crowd shouted, 'Let him be crucified!' They did so again even when Pilate asked them what it was that Jesus had done wrong.

Barabbas was released whilst Jesus was led away by the Roman soldiers. This may all have happened by 8.30am.

The soldiers dressed him in a purple robe and put a crown made of thorny twigs on his head. Speaking in Greek they mocked him saying: 'Hail, king of the Jews!' After he had been stripped, tied to a pillar and whipped he was allowed to dress before being led outside the walls of Jerusalem to Golgotha for crucifixion, a common Roman sentence.

Simon, a visitor from Libya, was hailed on the way and ordered to carry the wooden crossbeam weighing about 30lb and needed for the crucifixion.

On top of the high ground at Golgotha there were tall wooden posts and the crossbar was fixed to one to create a cross. After Jesus had declined a drink of vinegar and myrrh, he was stripped and nailed to the new cross by his hands and feet. Being crucified on either side were two robbers. The nails were expertly driven into the hands to prevent the bodies from falling off.

Mark suggests this was as early as 9am. The soldiers stuck a notice on top saying 'King of the Jews' and then threw dice to decide which of them should have first choice of the prisoner's garments.

He was mocked by some passers-by whilst Mary Magdalene and other women who had looked after him watched from nearby.

At 3pm, just before dying after maybe as long as six hours on the cross, he called out in Aramaic the first line of Psalm 22: 'My God, my God why have you forsaken me?'

A study of the Sudarium in Oviedo Cathedral (see below) suggests that the body of Jesus remained on the cross for another hour. Then the body was laid on its right side on the ground for about forty-five minutes. Nicodemus had arrived with myrrh for the body just as the Three Kings had brought myrrh at Jesus' birth in anticipation of this traumatic moment.

Joseph of Arimathea, who had obtained permission from the Roman governor to take care of the body, bought a large linen cloth. At 5pm the body was picked up and carried for about five minutes to a nearby tomb which belonged to Joseph. There it was wrapped in the cloth, possibly the Shroud of Turin, and myrrh was sprinkled on top. By 6pm darkness was approaching and Mary Magdalene saw the stone rolled across the tomb entrance.

A possible date often given for these events is Friday AD33 since this coincides with an eclipse of the moon which may have led St Peter to quote a passage about a blood moon (Acts 2.16-21) when recalling the crucifixion.

St Veronica

In the Bible there is no mention of St Veronica although the story of Christ leaving an impression of his face on a handkerchief offered by Veronica whilst he was carrying the cross has been depicted in many paintings. Today she is the patron of photographers. She may have first appeared as a character in open-air passion plays. It is only since the seventeenth century that Veronica has been included in the Stations of the Cross meditations. A century earlier St Charles Borromeo had such doubts about her authenticity that he banned her feast in his Milan diocese. On Good Friday 2007 Pope Benedict XVI dropped Veronica from the Stations of the Cross when he led the traditional meditation at the Colosseum.

A 6 x 9 inch cloth with the image of a face is at a monastery in Manoppello in Italy. This Veil of Veronica has the impression of a bloody face which is the exact dimensions of the one found on the Turin shroud.

Jaén Cathedral in Spain's Andalusia displays today, and every Friday morning, a cloth said to be Veronica's although it may be of similar status to the one which also has an image in the Monasterio de la Santa Faz (Monastery of the Holy Face) in the village of San Juan north of Alicante. This is a linen sheet claimed to have been used to wrap the cloth used by Veronica and it is the object of a huge pilgrimage on the second Thursday after Easter Day when families and groups visit and picnic outside. Another is shown in St Peter's in Rome and a related similar image is found at the Church of St Bartholomew of the Armenians in Genoa.

Veronica is derived from two Greek words meaning *true representation*.

Other Relics

The cross of the crucifixion, known as the True Cross, appears to have still existed in 326 when St Helena recorded seeing it in Jerusalem. Spanish pilgrim Egeria saw it later in the century. This was possibly only the crossbar as the upright stake remained permanently in the ground. About 350 Cyril of Jerusalem refers to fragments being dispersed around the Christian world and today many churches claim to have a piece of the cypress wood although authenticity is difficult to prove. The number of relics around the world would if put together only amount to a fraction of the massive cross. Heligenkreuz Abbey near Vienna has a large piece. The largest, a 24 inch long fragment with the nail hole for the left hand, is in the care of Franciscans at the remote Santo Toribio de Liébana monastery near Potes in Cantabria, northern Spain.

The chapel of Heritage Hall at Downham Market in Norfolk has a relic of the True Cross as does Caravaca de la Cruz in Spain. Rome's church of Sante Croce in Gerusalemme has several pieces along with a nail and a third object said to be the 'King of the Jews' notice fixed to the cross.

Also in Rome at Santa Pressede Church is part of a marble column said to be the one Christ was tied to for scourging. Another section is in St George's Cathedral Istanbul having been taken there by St Helena. Next to Rome's St John Lateran are the Holy Stairs brought from Jerusalem and believed to have been trodden by Christ at Pilate's building on the day of his crucifixion. Blood can be seen on one step.

A crown of thorns, missing its thorns but said to be the one placed on Jesus' head, is on view today from 10am to 5pm at Notre Dame in Paris where it has been since 1806. It was brought in 1239 to Paris where it was housed in the specially built Saint Chapelle. A thorn said to be from the crown is displayed this week in Stonyhurst College chapel in Lancashire and in Italy at Montone on Easter Monday and nearby Preggio on Easter Tuesday.

The loin cloth claimed as the one worn by Christ on the cross is in Aachen Cathedral although no longer on public view.

Bruges in Belgium has a relic claimed to contain a blood-stained cloth. In St Mark's Venice, a relic of the cross and a blood sample are brought from the treasury into the basilica at 9pm, which is about an hour after the Good Friday liturgy has finished.

Turin Cathedral in Italy has the famous Shroud and Oviedo Cathedral in Spain keeps the Sudarium which is exposed at the end of today's liturgy. (See Easter Day page 102.)

Trier Cathedral in Germany holds a robe said to be the seamless garment worn by Jesus before he was nailed to the cross. If genuine, and it has never been subjected to scientific analysis, it survives because the soldiers did not wish to tear it and instead cast lots (John 19.23). According to tradition, it was found in the twelfth century by St Helena who gave it to St Agricius, Archbishop of Trier. The first recorded public display was not until 1512. It was last exposed in 2012.

The Church of St Denis at Argenteuil in France, which appears in Monet's *Autumn in Argenteuil*, also has a coat claimed as the seamless robe. It existed in 1156 and some suggest that both are genuine with Argenteuil's being the undergarment.

In Church

The Triduum Part 2
Good Friday Liturgy
The liturgy is in four parts: readings, prayers, veneration of the cross and Holy Communion. This reflects the keeping of Good Friday in fourth-century Jerusalem as recorded by Egeria who saw a relic of the True Cross venerated.

The church including the altar is bare. The vestments are red.

The clergy enter and may prostrate themselves before the altar in recognition of the magnitude of Christ's action. There is a reading of St John's account of today whilst the congregation stands except for a pause to kneel at the point where Christ's death is recorded. This is followed by prayers for Church, state, Jews and unbelievers.

The entry of a cross in procession began in the fourth century when the Pope walked barefoot in procession from St John Lateran to Santa Croce in Gerusalemme where there is a relic of the True Cross. Then, as today in this service, the deacon holding the wooden cross sang: 'This is the wood of the cross.' Sometimes the cross is covered and gradually exposed in procession.

Depending on the size of the congregation there is usually an opportunity to individually touch or kiss the cross.

By the end of the liturgy, after Communion provided by the bread consecrated last night and watched in the vigil, there are two candles and the cross on the altar.

Suitable hymns include *My song is love unknown*, *When I survey the wondrous Cross* and *There is a green hill far away*. The latter, first published in 1848, was inspired by a hill outside the walled city of Derry which made the author C. F. Alexander think of Calvary.

By tradition, begun by Pope Paul V in 1618, the collection in Roman Catholic churches goes towards the upkeep of holy places in the Holy Land. The fund ensures that buildings remain accessible and local Christians remain in their homeland.

The congregation departs in silence as if onlookers at Calvary.

Three Hours Service

Many Anglican churches hold a service from 12 noon to 3pm to mark the known hours of Christ on the cross. Sometimes it is liturgical – including The Litany, matins and Ante-Communion or the Good Friday liturgy – but often it can be a series of addresses and hymns.

There is a record of a three-hour watch from 12 noon to 3pm at the crucifixion site in Jerusalem in 385. This Three Hours devotion was re-invented at Lima in Chile by Fr Alonso Messia in about 1687. It soon spread to neighbouring South American countries and to Rome where by 1818 it was observed by five churches including the Jesuit mother church. The Jesuits introduced it to their English churches in the nineteenth century. In 1864 it was adopted by Anglicans at the new St Alban's Holborn, where Fr Alexander Mackonochie was vicar, followed a year after by St Mary's Prestbury in Gloucestershire. St Paul's Cathedral first held a Three Hours in 1878 and Westminster Abbey in 1896.

The Three Hours was abruptly abandoned in 1956 by most Roman Catholic churches when the new Holy Week liturgy was introduced. The main Good Friday service now has to be held at a time between 12 noon and 9pm and most churches start at 3pm – the hour of Christ's death.

But St Alban's Holborn maintains the Three Hours starting at 12 noon with the Stations of the Cross followed by Allegri's Miserere (see below) and the day's main liturgy. St Paul's Cathedral continues to hold a Three Hours led by a notable preacher.

Stations of the Cross

The Stations of the Cross, which evolved in Europe with promotion by the Franciscans into fourteen depictions of Christ's last hours, provides the opportunity for a virtual pilgrimage.

The Miserere

The Miserere, a twelve-minute setting of Psalm 51 by Gregorio Allegri (1582-1652) often heard today, was composed about 1630 for *Tenebrae* (see page 66) and at first was only sung in the Vatican's Sistine Chapel. Its use spread after 1770 when the 14-year-old Mozart, on a visit with his father, memorised the twelve minute piece with the aid of notes on a piece of paper concealed in his hat. It was brought to England by music historian Dr Charles Burney and published in 1771. The version heard most now, and possibly based on embellishments, was produced in 1951 by Worcester Cathedral's former choirmaster Sir Ivor Atkins. But even the very modern setting by James MacMillan still owes a debt to Allegri.

In Jerusalem Today

Jerusalem's Holy Sepulchre Church covers the site of both the crucifixion and the tomb and here the Celebration of the Passion is at 8.15am before the Way of the Cross, along the route of Jesus' last walk before death, later in the morning. A burial procession is held in the evening at the Holy Sepulchre Church.

In Rome Tonight

The liturgy at St Peter's begins at 5pm as today is a working day in Italy. Later in the evening the Pope goes to the Colosseum to lead a candlelit Stations of the Cross in a tradition revived in 1964 by Pope Paul VI. The Roman amphitheatre was first used for the stations in 1750.

Good Friday Customs

Hot Cross Buns

It is claimed that the first cross-marked buns were made on Good Friday 1361 at St Albans Abbey (now cathedral) in Hertfordshire and distributed to the poor from the refectory door. (This stood to the south of the church.) Brother Thomas Rocliffe devised the secret recipe which is still held by the once abbey-owned Redbournbury Mill. Now around 3000 hot cross buns are made, using local organic wheat, for sale at the cathedral's Abbot's Kitchen during Holy Week. The recipe includes just a few currants but the mystery lies with the spices. The bun is supposed to contain 'grains of paradise' found in Africa and used in brewing, but today's substitute is cardamom. Both were probably brought to England by the Normans.

On Good Friday 1773 Samuel Johnson and James Boswell had tea and hot cross buns for breakfast at Bolt Court off Fleet Street before going to St Clement Danes and fasting for the rest of the day.

The Victorians increased the fruit content and introduced the distinctive paste cross in place of a simple cross which had been made made with a knife just before baking. As late as 1939 hot cross buns were delivered to homes early on Good Friday morning in Surrey. Although hot cross buns are now on sale all year round there is still a surge in sales just before Good Friday.

St Bartholomew-the-Great in London's Smithfield maintains the Butterworth Charity custom of distributing hot cross buns during a service in the churchyard before the main liturgy at noon. The rector stands on a tomb with baskets of buns at his feet. Once up to twenty-one poor widows of the parish could receive 6d and a hot cross bun. No widows came forward between 1973 and 2014 but everyone receives half a buttered bun. The service, which begins with a procession involving the choir, churchwardens and the verger, consists of a hymn, address, bun distribution and a final hymn during which there is a collection towards the Butterworth Charity. Law publisher Joshua Butterworth invested a sum in 1887 so that the custom dating from at least 1686 could be maintained.

Spices give a bun a long life such as one made in 1821 and now in the possession of the baker's great-great-great-granddaughter in Deeping St James, Lincolnshire. The oldest could be one in Colchester dated 1807.

At the Widow's Son Inn next to Devons Road Station in Bow, east London, a hot cross bun is added by a sailor to a collection hanging above the bar. A hanging string bag of buns kept for medicinal purposes was not uncommon. However, here it is claimed that more than two hundred years ago, possibly as early as the 1770s, a widow made some hot cross buns expecting her sailor son to return. Sailors often took one on a voyage as a lucky charm to prevent shipwreck. However, it was also not unusual for a few spare hot cross buns to be hung from the kitchen ceiling until needed for a sick person. The hard bun would be grated into hot milk. In 1848 the widow's cottage was replaced by the pub which retained the buns. The ceremony in the packed pub takes place at 3pm.

A similar custom is held at noon in The Bell at Horndon-on-the-Hill in Essex. When a new landlord took over on Good Friday 1906 he hung a hot cross bun on one of the medieval oak beams. Another was added every year and it has become the tradition for the oldest available person in the village to hang the new bun. The 1942 bun was made with concrete due to the wartime flour shortage and the 1991 one is wooden in honour of a 100th birthday. In 2006 the Bishop of Bradwell, a villager, tied the centenary bun to the beam. Around four hundred buns are given away.

Marbles

Marbles is a traditional Good Friday game in parts of Sussex and may be connected with the Roman soldiers playing with dice at the foot of the cross.

Games of marbles are played by over one hundred and twenty-five people at Battle in Sussex on Abbey Green this morning. Here the marbles custom, once Battle against nearby Nertherfield but now involving other teams, was restored in 1927 and since 1972 women as well as men take part.

At Tinsley Green, near Gatwick, Sussex, the British Marbles Championship is held at the Greyhound pub from 10am until about 4.30pm. The formal annual event, now involving over a hundred players, started here in 1932 although the game was being played in the village in at least 1588. The pub has a round ring outside with as many as nineteen teams competing including sometimes some from abroad. There are also three rings in the back garden. Spectators sit in a square round the main ring to watch the continuous play. Inside the pub there are photographs from past years including 1936, when a team from Reigate's London Country Bus garage won, and 1977, when Sealed Knot members played in Cavalier costume.

Skipping

At lunchtime on the road outside the wisteria-covered Rose Cottage pub in the Sussex village of Alciston in Sussex there is the Good Friday Sussex custom of skipping. At noon a long rope is swung by two people as singles, couples and entire families try out skipping whilst a crowd of about fifty watch. This is a direct remnant of the custom at nearby Brighton where fishermen, who did not fish on Good Friday, lent their ropes for skipping by children. The rope was associated with the rope used by Judas Iscariot to hang himself and today was known as Long Rope Day. The skipping was already an old custom when reported in 1863 and continued until the World War II when the seafront was closed and the custom transferred to Alciston.

Skipping on Good Friday morning also took place on Parker's Piece in Cambridge until the World War II.

Play

The Pace Egg play, dating from the 1500s and performed annually at Heptonstall in Yorkshire since it was revived in 1979 after a ten-year break, celebrates St George's triumphs over evil. Toss Pot, who adds to occasional comic asides, is a bumbling character who kisses girls in the crowd before presenting them with an egg. The four fifteen-minute performances are in Heptonstall's Weaver's Square. The nearby village of Midgley has its own ancient Pace Egg play about St George which is now performed by Calder High School pupils at least ten times today in the Calder Valley including Heptonstall, Hebden Bridge and Todmorden. Nearby Middleton has its play on Monday (see page 110).

Music

London's St Marylebone Church has a performance of Stainer's *The Crucifixion* this evening. Composer Sir John Stainer wrote the work for the church's choir in 1887 and it has been performed annually ever since. The words are by Stainer's friend Sparrow Simpson who at the time was curate at nearby Christ Church, Albany Street. The final hymn *All for Jesus, all for Jesus* soon became popular and now appears in hymn books.

Judas Figures

Portuguese and Spanish sailors are probably responsible for spreading the once widespread but now diminishing custom of burning a Judas figure today. The custom was strong in Athens and the Nigerian port of Calabar for example. It was common in Liverpool with the last recorded burning being in 1971. In 1964 the fire brigade had been called out just five times which was the lowest on record. Mexican artists Diego Rivera and Frida Kahlo both took a great interest in the creation of the cardboard Judas now considered important examples of their country's folk art. Today in Mexico a Judas, sometimes as tall as 20 feet, is joined by models of modern hate figures which are all usually burnt after being displayed.

Holy Saturday

Today is called either Holy Saturday or Easter Eve, but not Easter Saturday which is the Saturday *after* Easter Day. This is a common mistake made by shops and local authorities who have also begun to use the term Easter Friday for Good Friday.

Holy Saturday is a day of limbo, suspense and anticipation when the church is cleaned ready to celebrate Easter, beginning with the Easter Vigil tonight or very early tomorrow morning. The Church is waiting at the tomb but, since we know Christ's resurrection is coming, we prepare for Easter Day. With the Christian faith founded on Christ risen from the dead, tonight's service is the most important one in the year.

What Happened Today
Matthew 27.62-66

A guard was put on Jesus's tomb in addition to a seal for fear that the body would be removed and his death denied. To the disciples, today was the Sabbath when little took place. They must have been fearful of what might happen to them when the Passover week was over. We assume that they were disillusioned and scattered.

It is only tomorrow morning that they are hit by the astounding news that Jesus had risen from the dead (see Easter Day page 99).

Today in Jerusalem
Tonight a flame is brought out of the tomb in the Holy Sepulchre Church and met with shouts of 'Christ is risen!'. The light is passed beyond the building and taken long distances.

In Church

The Triduum Part 3

Easter Vigil

The Easter Vigil after dark is the climax of Lent, Holy Week and the Triduum. It is the transition of the week, the heart of the Christian Year and the fulfilment of Christmas. It is the moment when we recognise Christ's change from death to life. St Augustine called it 'the mother of all holy vigils'. John Paul II wrote: 'This is the Night above all nights, when keeping watch at Your grave we are the Church.'

The vigil begins with the congregation outside the church's west door and standing around a fire. This can be a brazier of wood or even, as at St Peter's Rome, a smokeless fuel.

The fire is the symbol for God as in the burning bush encountered by Moses. Five grains of incense looking like nails and representing the five wounds of Christ are pushed into the huge Easter candle before it is lit from the fire which also serves as a public announcement of Easter. At St Mary-on-the-Quay in Bristol it is deliberately lit between the portico's pillars to be clearly visible to those passing on foot or on a bus.

The congregation, by following the candle into church, is following Christ. Just two days after the deacon brought the cross into church and three times announced 'Behold the wood of the cross' so now the deacon holding the candle pauses three times to proclaim 'The light of Christ', the earliest known Christian chant.

Illuminated by each individual's candle lit from the great Easter candle, the people hear the Exsultet which is the proclamation of Christ's resurrection partly written by St Ambrose. The name comes from its first word which is *exult*. In Italy, especially Puglia as early as the eleventh century, this was read from an Exsultet roll which had dramatic upside down illustrations designed to be viewed the right way up by the congregation. As the long parchment, about 11 inches wide and sometimes around 22 feet long, gradually dropped down the front of the pulpit during the deacon's intoning of the message so the pictures were revealed.

Then follows according to ancient custom six Old Testament readings putting the resurrection in historical context.

The Gloria begins with the ringing of all the church bells inside and outside. At the Grosvenor Chapel in Mayfair it was customary as late as the 1970s for members of the congregation to bring their dinner bells along. St James's Piccadilly has invited people to 'bring any whistles, rattles, drums or other noise-making items to add to the celebration'.

The crosses will already have had their veils removed and now any statues covered with a purple cloth are uncovered.

The collect comes from the Gelasian Sacramentary, one of the oldest liturgical books dating from the eighth century, and includes the words stir up or *excita* which are heard in the even older Christ the King collect just before Advent.

A litany of saints is sung in procession to the font for baptisms or renewal baptismal promises. The litany can have a resonance as the names of Apostles are mingled with local saints.

During the vigil, the congregation moves out of death into joy as the service imperceptibly becomes the first Eucharist of Easter.

The climax sees the church reclaimed for the risen Christ with candles, decorations and his presence in the Blessed Sacrament.

From tonight the Alleluia, a Hebrew word meaning *Praise the Lord*, is added to some responses (see page 14).

This is the main Easter service with tomorrow's being an extra celebration or pastoral concession for those who cannot be at the vigil.

Development and Restoration of the Easter Vigil

The early Church, made up of some who had known the disciples, would meet on Easter Eve for a long vigil which included baptism of new members and the Eucharist at dawn on Easter morning. Partly because of old rules about not celebrating Mass after midday, the Easter Vigil was from about the fourteenth century held in daylight at around 9am on Saturday morning. Often there was only a small congregation and by Holy Saturday lunchtime it was Easter and the Lenten fast ended with the midday Angelus.

The German Liturgical Congress at Trier in June 1950 heard a call for change from a leading Catholic academic, Romano Guardini. This led to the German bishops asking the Vatican to move the vigil to the evening. As a result the ancient four-part vigil was restored to Saturday night in 1951 by the Roman Catholic Church.

Rome's Sacred Congregation of Rites indicated that the vigil should 'commence at such an hour that Mass will begin about midnight'. But the 1986 Anglican Lent, Holy Week and Easter prayer book encouraged the early morning option. The final verse of the vigil's Exsultet assumes that 'the Morning Star' will find the Easter candle 'still burning'.

The Easter Vigil on Saturday night allows for a proper climax to Holy Week at a proper hour. The Vigil is kept sometime in the darkness between Holy Saturday and Easter Day when Christ rose from the dead. Many Anglican cathedrals and churches now keep the vigil at the even more appropriate time of just before dawn on Easter Day (see Easter Day page 100) rather than shortly after dusk or just before midnight. A Saturday night vigil ending before midnight might be thought to pre-empt the great climax of the following day after a week when the other central events have been recalled at roughly the correct hour. However, a late night vigil celebrates the resurrection which took place during the night rather than anticipating the discovery of the event at dawn. The vigil in Anglo-Saxon Benedictine churches, such as Winchester Cathedral, included a brief liturgical drama of the tomb being found empty.

Around fifteen Anglican cathedrals in the British Isles and six central London churches opt for a dawn Easter Vigil. At whatever the hour, in many of the cathedrals new Christians are baptised and confirmed in keeping with the early Church custom.

Holy Saturday Traditions

Bacup, Lancashire

The Britannia Coconut Dancers, also known as the Nutters, have danced around Bacup since 1857 although the origin of this unique English ceremonial dance is very much older. At 9am the eleven-strong male and female team, accompanied by the Stacksteads Silver Band, starts off at the Traveller's Rest. The dancers with blackened faces dress in turban-like hats decorated with rosettes and coloured feathers, black jerseys, red and white skirts, white stockings and black leather Lancashire clogs. The nuts are the tops of cotton bobbins attached to the dancers and used to make rippling sounds. The garland and nut dances are said to have been brought by Moors to Cornwall and then taken to Lancashire by tin miners working in the coal pits. The blackened faces are said to be a connection with Moorish pirates seen in Cornwall, camouflage to make them anonymous or to recall the participation of coalminers. Mummers at Padstow in Cornwall have blackened faces. The original Bacup dancers were males who worked at the Royal Britannia Mill. Today the Coconutters dance pub to pub into Bacup in the morning and during the afternoon the dancers move pub to pub towards Stacksteads to finish at about 8pm outside The Glen.

Cyprus

Bonfires, often with a Judas figure on top, burn long after midnight in towns and villages despite attempts by Cypriot authorities to avoid fire risks in public places.

Poland and Russia

In Poland decorated baskets called *swieconka*, containing hard boiled eggs, a model sugar lamb to represent the traditional meat and other symbolic food, are taken to church this morning to be blessed, as are Easter cakes in Russia.

The Polish basket contains Easter Day breakfast and is covered with a white linen cloth representing the shroud of Christ.

EASTER

Easter Day

In the eighth century, the Venerable Bede suggested that the word *Easter* came from *Eostre*, a little known Saxon god. However, it is more likely that the word is related to *dawn* indicating the *start* of spring and new growth. Abroad the name for today is more appropriately usually derived from *Pesach*, which is the Hebrew word for *Passover*, hence *Pacques* in France, *Pascua* or *Pasqua* in Spain and Portugal, *Paach* in Holland, *Paques* and *Påsk* in Sweden.

Today is even more important than Christmas Day for Christianity is only credible because of what happened on Good Friday and early on the first Easter Day. Christ did not fail his followers even in the face of a terrible death. St Paul, writing to the church at Corinth said 'if Christ has not been raised, then our preaching is without substance' (1 Corinthians 15.14).

The events of today were the beginning of a long process during which the disciples regained their confidence. The resurrection of Christ was proof that, after all the doubts, there was life after death and good could triumph over evil. In death life is not ended but changed. God has power over life and death. Jesus was and is God.

What Happened Today
Matthew 28.1-15; Mark 16.1-18; Luke 24.1-49; John 20.1-26

Dawn
It was still dark when Mary Magdalene Mary who was mother of Apostle St James the Less, and Joanna arrived at the tomb with spices to anoint the body of Christ. They had been wondering

who would move the stone at the entrance and maybe hoping that the guards would do so for them. At this moment just before first light there may have been an earthquake or at least the noise of the stone being rolled back. Maybe the earthquake moved the stone. This seems to have frightened the guard ordered to stand outside.

When Mary Magdalene realised that the stone had already been rolled back she turned away. Soon after she saw Peter and John who were also on their way and she ran towards them warning that Christ's body seemed to have been removed. The two shocked disciples started running to the tomb. John made it there first and looking through the opening saw the linen cloths which had been wrapped round the body folded up on the floor. When Peter arrived he went straight in and found the cloth which had been put over the head. Then incredulous John went inside as the two realised that Jesus' warnings had been true.

When the two shocked disciples left then Mary, who had remained crying outside, also went inside. She saw two angels sitting where the body of Jesus had been. They asked why she was crying. 'They have taken my Lord away, and I don't know where they have put him', she said turning to go. She was confronted by another figure whom she mistook for the gardener. As she pleaded to be told where the body had been taken, the man spoke revealing himself as Christ by saying in his familiar voice 'Mary'. 'Master', she replied in recognition as he warned her not to embrace him as he was not yet ascended to heaven.

'Go and find my brothers,' he requested. 'and tell them: I am ascending to my Father and your Father, to my God and your God.'

The Ascension (see page 127) would happen before the summer. Meanwhile Mary went to find the others who, of course, did not believe her.

Afternoon

During the afternoon two disciples, not members of the remaining Eleven but Cleophas and another who may have been his wife

Mary, were walking from Jerusalem towards Emmaus seven miles away. (The village is probably the place now known as El-Qubeibeh although Motza-Kolonia, three and a half miles west of Jerusalem, was recently identified by Professor Carsten Thiede as a likely location. Abu Ghosh, which has a Benedictine abbey called St Mary of the Resurrection, also claims to be authentic location.) A stranger joined them who appeared to know nothing of the recent events in Jerusalem involving their leader, Jesus. The two recounted their experiences and then the stranger recalled all the Old Testament passages which foretold these events. They asked their interesting and sympathetic companion to join them at an inn rather than press on alone. At the table the stranger took bread, blessed it and handed it to them. He disappeared as the two realised that Christ had been with them.

Although it was the end of the day they raced back to Jerusalem arriving almost certainly at least by early evening to tell the Eleven inner group of disciples. Still they did not believe that Jesus had appeared even though he may have risen from the dead.

Evening

In the evening in Jerusalem ten of the original twelve were gathered behind closed doors. Thomas was elsewhere and we must assume that Judas, if he had not already committed suicide, was keeping away from his former colleagues. Jesus appeared amongst them saying 'Peace be with you'. He showed them his injured hands and side before saying: 'Peace be with you. As the Father sent me, so am I sending you.'

He anticipated Pentecost (page 140) by breathing on them saying 'Receive the Holy Spirit. For those whose sins you forgive they are forgiven; for those whose sins you retain they are retained' (see page 62). Then they watched him eat a piece of their grilled fish.

Late night or later

When Thomas heard about Christ's appearance from the others he remained doubtful, refusing to believe anything unless he could touch the wounds himself.

Relics

The main linen cloth found folded in the tomb may be the Turin Shroud in Italy's Turin Cathedral. Tests suggest that the outline of the body found on the cloth is the result of radiation linked to the resurrection. The marks of the knees and nose have traces of soil consistent with a fall whilst carrying the cross. There is also evidence of whipping, traces of human sweat and blood, myrrh and pollen from plants which grew in Jerusalem. The Shroud was described by Pope John Paul II as 'a mirror of the gospel'.

The Holy Chamber at Spain's Oviedo Cathedral has the Oviedo Cloth (El Santo Sudario) which may be the 'the cloth that had been over his head' (John 20:6) – tied round the top of the head and under the chin to keep the mouth closed which is why there is a gap between the front and back heads on the Shroud image. This is the cloth found by Peter. Tests indicate that the blood on both objects is from the same group and both had been in contact.

A piece of the stone doorway which was found rolled back is preserved in today's Chapel of the Angel at the entrance to the tomb in the Holy Sepulchre.

In Church

Dawn Vigil

A dawn Easter Vigil gives members of the congregation the opportunity to get up early to meet the risen Lord at the hour when the first visitors arrived at the tomb. The gospel reading about the discovery of the empty tomb at this time has greater resonance. Rochester Cathedral has observed the vigil at dawn since 1993 with growing numbers attending within three years. But it is not always popular with non-churchgoers. There were complaints in Bruton in Somerset when rockets were set off during the 6am champagne and bacon sandwich breakfast which followed the Vigil at St Mary's.

In Ireland around thirty parishes maintain the tradition of celebrating an early outdoor Mass, often in a cemetery, at 6am or 7am.

Main Morning Mass
This is in addition to the Vigil but those who received Communion last night may do so again.

Easter Sunday Evening Mass
At the evening Mass there is provision for the story of Jesus meeting disciples on the road to Emmaus to be the gospel reading. Those who have experienced the Vigil Mass during the night but still intend being also at a daytime Eucharist may wish to attend a second celebration at the end of the day.

A suitable hymn for tonight is *Abide with me* which was inspired by the words of the two disciples at Emmaus: 'Abide with us: for it is toward evening, and the day is far spent' (Luke 24.29 in the King James version familiar to hymn writer Henry Francis Lyte in 1847).

Evening Prayer
Tonight, in the Roman Evening Prayer, the antiphon of the Magnificat (which is first heard from Mary when Jesus is conceived) says: 'On the evening of that Sunday, when the disciples were gathered behind locked doors, Jesus came and stood among them. He said to them, Peace be with you, alleluia.'

Other Hymns
Suitable hymns include *This joyful Eastertide* by George Woodward, vicar of Walsingham, who also wrote *Ding-dong! Merrily on high!* for Christmas. *The day of Resurrection! Earth tell it out abroad* by J. M. Neale is based on words from the matins of Easter Day in the Orthodox Church.

Today in the Holy Land
At El-Qubeibeh there is at 4.30pm, about the hour Christ revealed himself to the two disciples, a short ceremony.

Easter Food and Symbols

Eggs

Hard-boiled eggs feature in the Passover meal when guests mash them into the salted water representing the Red Sea which the Hebrews crossed. So the egg continues to represent new life with the chick bursting out as did Christ from the tomb. During the fourth century eggs were forbidden in Lent and by the Middle Ages an Easter Day treat was hard-boiled eggs with a green herb sauce. Edward I had 450 eggs coloured for the court at Easter 1290. A fresh egg remained an Easter treat into the twentieth century with hens in Britain laying mainly in spring and summer.

Eggs and Chocolate

Eggs and chocolate came together in Germany in the early nineteenth century. In England Fry's of Bristol made the first chocolate Easter egg in 1873 followed by Cadbury's in 1875. Both were plain chocolate. Cadbury's Milk Chocolate egg did not appear until 1905. Cadbury's Creme Egg was introduced in 1923 although the small foil-wrapped Creme Egg, which sells over 200 million a year, was not made until 1971. In France chocolate fish, representing the early Christian symbol, are as familiar as the eggs.

Easter Hare

Hares, found in decorations of West Country churches and Paderborn Cathedral in Germany, have been a symbol of fertility and long life at least since ancient Egyptian times. Because hares were believed to produce without sexual intercourse they became associated with the Virgin Mary.

Rabbits, once mainly found in Spain and France, were brought to England by the Normans who built rabbit warrens for obtaining fur and food. The first documented use of the bunny as a symbol of Easter appears in Germany in the sixteenth century although the actual matching of the holiday and the hare was probably a much earlier folk tradition. Not surprisingly, it was also the Germans who made the first chocolate Easter bunnies in the nineteenth century.

Italian Andrea Mantegna's *Agony in the Garden*, painted about 1460 and now in London's National Gallery, shows what appear to be rabbits, or hares, in the Garden of Gethsemane.

(See Hare Pie Scrambling, page 108.)

Lambs

The traditional food at lunchtime is lamb. This is the main dish at the Jewish Passover and so was possibly eaten at the Last Supper (see page 70). In the Christian tradition Christ is the Lamb of God and in northern Europe spring lamb is fortunately easily available at Easter time. Hence the spring lambs on the Easter cards.

Easter Day Customs

London

The dawn Easter Vigil at St Bride's Fleet Street is followed by egg rolling in Fleet Street which runs gently downhill towards the River Fleet valley. The custom began in 1987 when vicar Canon John Oates persuaded the congregation to follow the example of his previous church in Richmond. The early morning vigil has become a popular Fleet Street tradition.

Bristol

Egg rolling has taken place in Vale Street which is Europe's steepest residential hill since 1995. The contest is to see whose egg rolls the furthest. Afterwards the gutter is full of broken coloured eggs.

Urbi et Orbi Blessing

Since 1985 Holland has supplied the flowers on the steps of St Peter's for the main morning Mass in Rome's St Peter's Square. Afterwards at noon the Pope delivers an Easter Message from St Peter's central balcony and gives the blessing, Urbi et Orbi, to the city and the world. The custom dates only from 1922 when the new mass media enabled a message to be spread quickly. Today many countries take the live broadcast.

Florence's Exploding Cart

The *Scoppio del Carro*, meaning *explosion of the cart*, takes place outside Florence Cathedral this morning. The cart arrives pulled by four white oxon. Before the 10.30am Solemn Mass, the archbishop and cathedral clergy process to the front of the baptistry, a separate building opposite the west door, to receive the holy fire. The flame is brought in a procession of costumed figures from Santi Apostoli Church where the flame is created by using three stones from Jerusalem's Holy Sepulchre. In the cathedral, as the archbishop intones the Gloria, the deacon uses this flame to light a fuse near the sanctuary which sends a dove-shaped rocket down a wire, running the length of the nave out the west door, triggering smoke and fireworks in the 32 foot high cart. The dove returns at once at speed as bells ring out during the display lasting about eight minutes. Despite its name, the special cart remains intact to be used next year. This custom dates from at least 1494 although until 1957, when new Easter services were introduced, it took place at 12 noon on Holy Saturday with the flame taken from the Easter candle.

Easter Monday

Today has been an official holiday only since the 1871 Bank Holidays Act which made bills due on Easter Monday to be due on Tuesday instead. It also laid down that a person could not be made to do anything that he or she could not be made to do on the common law holidays of Christmas Day and Good Friday. Prior to this time banking continued today although some enterprises took a holiday.

This is very much part of the beginning of the forty-day Easter season. Even the Book of Common Prayer has a collect and readings for today.

Easter Monday Customs

Egg Rolling

Egg rolling is said to represent the stone being rolled back from Christ's tomb. It has been a custom at Preston in Lancashire since the 1870s when the day was a new Bank Holiday. In the afternoon children would arrive at Avenham Park overlooking the River Ribble with baskets filled with hard-boiled eggs which had been decorated in different colours. The tradition is strongly maintained by families and more recently it has become the custom to roll chocolate eggs down the steep slope.

The tradition of the Easter Monday morning egg roll on the South Lawn of the White House in Washington began in 1878.

Biddenden Maids, Dole

At Biddenden in Kent around eighty elderly people qualify under the 800-year-old Biddenden Maids' Charity to collect two 4lb loaves, 1lb of cheese and 1lb tea from a window of the Old Workhouse. This stands along with allotments on Bread and Cheese Land bequeathed by the Siamese twins Eliza and Mary Chulkhurst, born in 1100 and known as the Biddenden Maids. The twins lived to the age of 34 when they died within six hours of each other. The earliest record of the Easter distribution which was originally in church is a 1605 archdeacon's visitation. Over the next three centuries there are constant reports of disorder as visitors tried to obtain the dole. In the 1770s a thousand distinctive oblong biscuits showing the twins' image were thrown from the church roof to the crowd on Easter Day. In 1882 the Archbishop of Canterbury banned the beer which has been replaced by a packet of tea. At the end of the nineteenth century the venue was changed to the workhouse and the day to Easter Monday. Once pensioners brought pillow cases to carry their dole but now the items are presented in recycled carrier bags. All 'strangers and parishioners' calling at the window this morning receive one of the hard and scarcely edible flour and water biscuits depicting the twins. Rents fund the gifts.

Hare Pie Scrambling

Hare Pie Scrambling and Bottle Kicking is claimed to have taken place today at Hallaton in Leicestershire for at least 800 years. The fine church, in the county's prettiest village, is the setting for the 11am service which begins with the rector receiving three small barrels (called bottles) of beer, two sacks for pies, a basket of penny loaves and the warrener's staff topped with the image of a hare. The items are placed before the high altar and collected at the end by the leading participants. The priest preaches a sermon for which a payment of one shilling (five pence) is later made.

Crowds build up by lunchtime when at 1.45pm a hare pie is carried in procession with a band from The Fox pub down to the church gates. After the pie has been blessed, portions are handed out by the rector while others help to throw pieces to those at the back of the always large crowd to create the first of two hare pie scrambles. Some of the pie goes into the two sacks. Afterwards all process to the Buttercross on the green where the rector ties ribbons on the bottles and seals the sacks with more ribbon. Here the two dozen penny loaves for the poor are thrown to the crowd. Afterwards the company returns to The Fox.

Immediately the procession turns round to begin the trip back past the green and church and up Bride Hill for the start of Bottle Kicking at 3pm on Hare Pie Bank. The last pieces of hare pie are thrown to the crowd from the sacks for the final hare pie scramble. Bottle kicking is a rough game like Shrove Tuesday football and begins once the third bottle has been thrown in the air and hit the ground. There are few rules and participants from Hallaton or nearby Medbourne simply have to get this bottle across their boundary stream. The late Paul Daisley MP once won for Hallaton. When a bottle (full of ale) is won the second bottle – a colourful dummy and so lighter – is brought into play. Only if the same side wins is the third bottle brought into play. When the game ends, sometimes after several hours, the victorious side celebrates by opening a bottle at the Buttercross. In 2011 there were twenty casualties including players with a neck injury and a broken collar bone.

William Webb Ellis, inventor of rugby, stayed as a child with his uncle who was rector of Hallaton.

The hare has long been associated with Easter (see page 104). The direct route to Hare Pie Bank, first recorded as a place name in 1698, is along a path beginning at an unmarked doorway in the main street. This footpath, called Tenters, was once Chapel Way leading to a thirteenth-century St Morrell's Chapel which was on Hare Pie Bank until around 1590. St Morrell, or Maurilius of Angers, is said to have lived in the area in the fifth century.

It is unclear how the pie scrambling and bottle kicking, first recorded in 1796, came together but occasional efforts to end the custom have always failed. Indeed the distribution of bread which ceased in the 1890s was revived in the 1960s and now the pie is once again made with real hare. Around 4000 to 5000 people attend the event.

Pace Egg Play

Middleton in Yorkshire had a Pace Egg play (see page 89) in the nineteenth century which was revived in 1967 by comedian Mike Harding with as many as seventeen twenty-minute performances featuring the battle between the Turkish knight and St George who triumphs. There are now just seven stops at half hour intervals outside pubs starting at The Dusty Miller from about 12.30pm. The day ends at about 4pm with egg rolling on the slope next to the church.

Rome

In Italy today is known as Monday of the Angel because of the angel at the tomb yesterday. The Pope appears at his window in St Peter's Square to lead the *Regina Caeli* which at Easter replaces the Angelus.

Holy Land

In the basilica at El-Qubeibah, the village near Jerusalem believed to be Emmaus, there is a Pontifical Mass this morning. The church is close to a stretch of Roman road which may be the Jerusalem-Emmaus road walked by the risen Christ on the first Easter Day.

Second Sunday of Easter
Low Sunday
Divine Mercy Sunday

Low comes from *Laudes* (meaning praise) which was once sung as the sequence *Laudes Salvatori voce modulemur supplici* (Let us sing Alleluia Alleluia praises to the Saviour with humble voice) before today's gospel. The popular name Low Sunday may have endured simply because this Sunday is 'back to a normal Sunday' and a contrast to last Sunday which was the high day of the year. It can also be a 'low' Sunday because so many of the regular members of the congregation and the clergy are away on holiday. But Easter continues and there are plenty of Alleluias after responses and at the gospel acclamation. We are still living in real time the events in Jerusalem and today's gospel reading is always the account (John 20:19-31) of what happened on the first Low Sunday.

In 1970 the official name of this Sunday became the Second Sunday of Easter although it also enjoys other names.

Divine Mercy Sunday
Since Millennium Year this Sunday has also been known as Divine Mercy Sunday due to the wish of Pope John Paul II. This followed the canonisation on Low Sunday 2000 of Polish St Faustina Kowalska who, between 1930 and her death in 1938, claimed to have received revelations from Christ on the Divine Mercy. She maintained that Jesus wished today to be Divine Mercy Sunday. At the time there were reservations about private revelations and as late as 1959 the Vatican condemned her writings and diary *Divine Mercy in my Soul* as unsound.

John Paul, who had presided at her beatification on Low Sunday 1993, heard the Mass of Divine Mercy Sunday celebrated in his room just over an hour before his death late on Easter Saturday in 2005. His last message, read afterwards, was: 'To all of mankind, who so often seems lost and dominated by the power of evil, egoism and fear, the Risen Lord offers as a gift His love which pardons, reconciles and opens the soul again to hope. It is a love that converts hearts and gives peace. How the world needs to understand and welcome Divine Mercy!'

John Paul's own beatification ceremony took place on Divine Mercy Sunday 2011 and his canonisation on the same Sunday in 2014.

Quasimodo Sunday
Another name for today is Quasimodo Sunday after the entrance antiphon at Mass which in Latin begins *Quasi modo geniti infantes* meaning *Like newborn infants* (1 Peter 2.2). In Victor Hugo's novel, *Notre-Dame de Paris*, the hunchback is called Quasimodo because when a child he was found abandoned in the cathedral porch on Quasimodo Sunday.

In Albis Sunday
A now very little used name is *in Albis* Sunday meaning *in white* and referring to converts received into the Church at the Easter Vigil now laying aside their white garment.

St Thomas Sunday
The Orthodox Church calls today Thomas Sunday because St Thomas saw the risen Christ today.

What Happened Today
John 20.26-29
This evening, as last Sunday, the Apostles were together in the same room in Jerusalem. The doors were closed but Jesus again appeared amongst them. 'Peace be with you,' he said and turned to Thomas who was missing this time a week ago. 'Put your

finger here; look, here are my hands. Give me your hand; put it into my side. Do not be unbelieving any more but believe.'

'My Lord and my God!' said Thomas. Jesus said: 'You believe because you can see me. Blessed are those who have not seen and yet believe.'

In Church

Today and on all Sundays in Easter the priest may sprinkle the congregation with water as a reminder of baptism and to emphasise that this is still Easter.

The first reading on this and the five Sundays during Easter is from the Acts of the Apostles instead of the Old Testament.

An evening Mass today has extra resonance in view of the evening appearance of Christ in the upper room. A suitable hymn is *Blessed Thomas, doubt no longer* by George B. Timms.

Third Sunday of Easter

Easter Day to the Ascension is, like Lent, a forty-day period. Sunday Masses between Low Sunday and Rogation Sunday (Sixth Sunday of Easter) continue to have an Easter feel. Recalled during this period are further resurrection appearances of Christ which helped to give the Apostles and disciples confidence.

What Happened Around This Time
Matthew 28.16-20 and John 21.1-25
The angel in the tomb had told the eleven disciples to go to Galilee and after at least a week they gathered on the mountain where Jesus had arranged to meet them. Some knelt down and Jesus came over to speak to them. 'All authority in heaven and on earth has been given to me', he declared before asking them to look beyond their own land to a worldwide Christian family. 'Go, therefore, make disciples of all nations; baptise them in the name of the Father and of the Son and of the Holy Spirit, and teach them to observe all the commands I gave you. And look, I am with you always; yes, to the end of time.' The mountain may have been the very high hill, the Mount of the Beatitudes overlooking the Sea of Galilee, where Jesus had preached the Sermon on the Mount.

Later Jesus appeared unexpectedly to seven of the Eleven when they were fishing early in the morning on the Sea of Galilee. Peter, Thomas (who had earlier doubted the resurrection), James, John, possibly Bartholomew and two others were on board about 100 yards out. Jesus stood on the shore.

'Haven't you caught anything, friends?' called Jesus who had not been recognised. They had nothing despite sailing since dawn but Jesus told them to try the net on the other side of the boat. Suddenly it was heavy with fish and John realised that the person on the shore was Christ. Peter plunged into the water and swam to him. Already there was a charcoal fire burning and bread. The catch amounted to a hundred and fifty-three fish and together they breakfasted.

Afterwards Jesus indicated that Peter was to be the leader and that it would cost him his life. Jesus asked him to follow and he did, even to being crucified like his master.

The beach breakfast is believed to have been at Tabgha which is a very short distance from the probable site of the Feeding of the 5000, with bread and fish, just a year before. Today the shore remains a stony beach with a little church built over the rock on which Jesus may have prepared breakfast.

Fourth Sunday of Easter
Good Shepherd Sunday

Today's gospel reading has had the theme of the Good Shepherd since 1474. It is always from John 10 (1-10, 11-18 or 27-30) where Jesus is the shepherd who lays down his life for his sheep. Bishops, successors to the Apostles, carry a shepherd's crook to signify their office and role.

Today is World Day of Prayer for Vocations which began in 1963 at the instigation of Pope Paul VI during the Second Vatican Council.

In Church

Prayers are said for vocations both to the priesthood and religious life and also to the caring professions such as nursing and teaching. *Vocation* means *sacrifice* and *laying self-interest aside for others*.

ROGATION

Sixth Sunday of Easter

Rogation Sunday
Cantate Sunday

Rogation comes from the Latin word *rogare* meaning *to ask* which was once part of today's gospel reading (John 16.24) and included the words 'Ask and you will receive'. By long tradition at this time God's blessing is asked for on the crops to be harvested later in the year. Rogation looks towards harvest festival in October.

Clergy and congregation sometimes process outside to pray for a good harvest and in some places also beat the bounds of the parish. Coastal parishes tend to pray for a good harvest of fish. Rogationtide lasts until Wednesday.

Cantate Sunday

Cantate Sunday, once a more widely used name, comes from the entrance antiphon at the start of Mass: *Cantate Domino novum canticum* meaning *Sing to the Lord a new song* (Psalm 96).

Beating the Bounds

In England Rogation processions round the parish date from the early eighth century having originated at Vienne in France about 470. The cross led the procession including clergy vested in copes whilst villagers helped to carry any saints' relics kept in the church. Stops were made to read the Gospel or say prayers for good crops. Some villages still have an old oak tree known as the Gospel Tree or Holy Tree where the pause was made for the Bible reading. Gospel Oak in north London is named after the now felled oak tree which stood in Southampton Road on the boundary of St Pancras and Hampstead parishes. A litany would be sung and bells rung as the procession moved from point to point. It was often the custom to head the procession with a dragon image which in the Ascension Day procession next Thursday would be relegated to the back with the cross at the front as a sign of the victory of Christianity over the forces of evil.

In time the Rogation procession was combined with, or evolved into, beating the bounds of the parish (see page 133) which involves going in procession to the boundary stones to check that they remain in place and ceremonially beat them with willow wands. Many once believed that beating the bounds drove evil spirits out of the community. Some Beating the Bounds ceremonies are held next Thursday to coincide with the Ascension.

Boundary stones can be in surprising places such as shops or pubs. On the rare occasion when the Queen's Chapel of the Savoy beats the bounds of London's Savoy Precinct it is necessary for the choirboys to go on the stage at the Lyceum Theatre to find one of the twelve boundary stones.

In the 1630s poet George Herbert commended Rogation and beating the bounds believing that neighbours walking together would reconcile their differences whilst giving thanks for the fruits of the field and preserving bounds.

Originally Rogation was observed tomorrow, or on Tuesday or Wednesday but in 1944 Bishop George Bell of Chichester issued a pastoral letter encouraging the observance of Rogation Sunday 'now happily chosen by the Minister of Agriculture as Farm Sunday'.

Rogation Sunday Events
Cambridge
Little St Mary's beats its parish bounds following the Solemn Mass. The route involves part of the town, following water courses and crossing both the River Cam and Fen Causeway.

Leighton Buzzard, Bedfordshire
The Wilkes Walk takes place following the Sunday morning

Parish Eucharist at All Saints. A garland bearer, crucifer, choir, clergy, charity trustees, churchwardens lead the congregation through the town to Wilkes Almshouses in North Street. The town crier walks ahead announcing the ceremony. On arrival there is an anthem before a choirboy or choirgirl stands on his or her head whilst part of a will is read by the Wilkes charity clerk. A cushion is provided for the head and the rector holds the feet. This is followed by prayers.

The charity dates from 1611 with the original almshouses for eight poor women being built by Edward Wilkes in 1630 in memory of his father John. They were endowed by grandson Matthew whose own will stated that at Rogationtide a child should be upended outside the almshouses during a reading of his father's will.

On the way back a stop is made at the market cross where children in the choir enjoy free buns and lemonade. Ale and 2000 spiced buns were given out to onlookers until 1896 when the scramble for free refreshment became too unseemly. Then the choir children received two shillings and sixpence each. Now the fee paid is £1.

The custom, which took place on Rogation Monday until 2011, began in 1693 when the processional route was longer. In 2013 it coincided with the town's May Fayre.

London

Beating the Bounds, recorded as an important annual Southwark event in 1536, was revived by Southwark Cathedral in 2004. A procession sets out after the morning Sung Eucharist on a route which can involve a boat trip along the parish boundary in the Thames. Inland there are several stops to beat the ground and chalk a special mark on buildings or pavements. Such marks have lingered on a Bankside wall near Shakespeare's Globe for years.

Mudeford, Dorset

This afternoon there is a blessing of waters from a rowing boat in Mudeford Run at the entrance to Christchurch Harbour. The choir and congregation of All Saints Church arrive in procession on Mudeford Quay for the twenty-five-minute service. The priest, sitting on a lobster pot, is rowed into the fast water to first bless and then hurl a silver cross into the water. It remains at the bottom of the Run with its many predecessors. Prayers are said for the safety of all fishermen and for a good harvest from the sea. The custom dates from 1930. Once the first salmon of the season was presented to the prior of Christchurch.

Southwell

The congregation of Southwell Minster, which has a window commemorating the planting nearby of the original Bramley apple tree, goes in procession along country lanes led by the choir, with three pauses for prayers, readings and blessing crops, to the agricultural school on Nottingham Trent University's Brackenhurst campus.

Rogation Wednesday
Eve of the Ascension

Today in Jerusalem
Roman Catholic Vespers at the Chapel of the Ascension (see below) on the Mount of Olives at 2.45pm is attended by Christians of other denominations who erect altars and tents in the walled courtyard in the care of Muslims. An Orthodox Vespers follows.

Custom
Planting Whitby's Penny Hedge
The Penny Hedge at Whitby in Yorkshire is planted at 9am on a beach known as Abraham's Bosom in the Upper Harbour. The very short hedge, or horngarth, is a fence made of nine hazel stakes woven together by thin branches. Penny is derived from penance and the hedge must withstand three tides. When building is complete at about 9.15am then a horn is sounded and the bailiff of the Fyling Court Leet shouts: 'Out upon ye, out upon ye, out upon ye.'

The custom dates from 1148 and probably began not as a penance but as an annual obligation of Whitby Abbey tenants to build a long fence down to the beach to contain grazing cattle. The bailiff represents the abbot of Whitby Abbey which was dissolved in 1539 and the horn is said to have belonged to the abbey. The custom is mentioned in Walter Scott's poem *Marmion*. Now that the River Esk tidal flow has been reduced the hedge often survives for the year and can be seen at low tide below the commemorative stone almost opposite the Middle Earth Tavern. On the very rare occasion when there is a high tide at 9am on

Ascension Eve, as in 1948 and 1981, a new hedge is not erected.

The mayor is present but, although there is again growing interest, the crowd is not yet as large as in the 1930s.

ASCENSION

Ascension Day
Thursday after Sixth Sunday of Easter

Ascension Day is the spiritual climax of the year and of the Annunciation (page 187). The creed said every Sunday includes the words 'he ascended into heaven and is seated on the right hand of God'.

Today marks Christ's last resurrection appearance to the disciples who report seeing him ascend. St Paul says that Christ had been seen by more than five hundred men and women between resurrection and ascension (1 Corinthians 15.6). His earthly task was complete and the leadership was passing to the Apostles.

Although Ascension Day is now largely ignored in Britain it is a public holiday in Austria, Belgium, Denmark, France, Germany, Luxembourg, Finland, Holland, Norway, Serbia, Sweden and Switzerland. Some Anglicans in England, Wales and Ireland and certain US provinces, but not New York, have followed France and Italy by observing the festival on the following Sunday. Vatican City celebrates today in advance of Italy.

In Britain there are a huge number of old customs which remind us of how important the day used to be in the life of the country. The Turners' Company 1604 charter, for example, lays down that the annual election of the new Master and Wardens shall take place today. Other City of London livery companies holding services include pattenmakers and parish clerks. City workers are reminded that it is Ascension Day by the sound of Bow Bells echoing down Cheapside and filling Bow Lane with sound for forty-five minutes before St Mary-le-Bow's lunchtime Mass.

In the Middle Ages a cross or statue of Christ was sometimes hauled on to the church roof to symbolise the Ascension.

The first record of tower top singing on Ascension Day to symbolise the ascension is at New College Oxford early in the seventeenth century. Inspired by Oxford May tower singing (see page 200) Hurstpierpioint College in Sussex introduced a hilltop celebration. Bloxham village school in Oxfordshire sang from the top of St Mary's Church tower from 1860. As children, Alan Bennett and Barbara Taylor Bradford both climbed the tower of Christ Church, Upper Armley on Ascension Day.

In 2009 Portsmouth Cathedral choir sang from the top of the city's 558 foot high Spinnaker Tower giving the 'highest performance in the UK' of Thomas Weelkes' *Alleluia, I heard a voice from heaven*. The following year St Peter's Bournemouth choir sang from a balloon.

What Happened Today
Luke 24.50-53 and Acts 1.4-11

Jesus appeared to the Eleven who were probably in the same upper room as before. He warned of the coming events of Pentecost by telling them to stay in Jerusalem and adding 'not many days from now, you are going to be baptised with the Holy Spirit'. They were to be his witnesses throughout the world.

Jesus then led these closest disciples out to the Mount of Olives. There he raised his hands to bless them and as he did so he was lifted up and disappeared into the cloud. As the amazed followers stared at the sky, two mysterious men in white (as at the tomb on Easter Day) stood nearby. 'Why are you Galileans standing here looking into the sky?' they asked. 'This Jesus who has been taken up from you into heaven will come back in the same way as you have seen him go to heaven.'

Afterwards the disciples walked back to the upper room where they joined Mary, mother of Jesus, his cousins and women disciples in continuous prayer. They knew that they would not meet Christ again on earth in any more resurrection experiences. But they were not really prepared for Pentecost (see page 139).

Although St Luke recorded in his gospel and the Acts of the Apostles that the Ascension came forty days after Easter there was in later years some argument about the length of time between the resurrection and ascension and whether Luke literally meant forty days or just a long time. In 400AD the Council of Toledo accepted the forty days report as correct.

The Ascension Site

The site of the Ascension, the highest point in Jerusalem, is now occupied by the tiny round Mosque of the Ascension, also known as the Chapel of the Ascension. It was first a Crusader Church built about 1150 and then acquired in 1198 by Muslims. The stone floor has a mark claimed as the footprint of Christ. Across the road is the Church of the Pater Noster on the site where Jesus taught the Lord's Prayer. This spot has long been thought to be possibly where Jesus spoke to his Apostles just before he ascended.

In Church

There is no clear indication about the time of day when the Ascension took place but many church services are held early in the morning.

Until recently the pascal candle, representing the risen Christ, was extinguished during the gospel reading at the point where Jesus ascends. Now the candle remains lit at services until Pentecost as a reminder that Christ remained with the Apostles through the Holy Communion. Also, the Easter season continues for another ten days until Pentecost (see page 139) in a few days' time.

Common Worship begins and ends the Eucharist with readings from the Acts of the Apostles. Immediately before the blessing there is an anticipation of coming Pentecost (see page 139).

Suitable hymns are *Hail the day that sees him rise*, *Alleluia* and *The head that once was crowned with thorns*. The Ascension anthem *God is gone up* by Gerald Finzi, with words by Edward Taylor (1642-1729), has been popular since first heard in 1951 at the musicians' church St Sepulchre's Newgate.

Today at the Ascension Site

There are Masses from midnight and a solemn Mass at 5.30am. Other services are held during the morning by the Armenian, Coptic, Greek Orthodox and Syrian Churches.

ASCENSION CUSTOMS

Tower Top Singing

St Andrew's in Cheddar, Somerset, started in the 1880s; St John's College Cambridge 1902, St Mary's Warwick 1907 and Southwell Minster in 2008. The growing tradition has also long been observed by Gloucester Cathedral, York Minster, Sherborne Abbey, Community of the Resurrection at Mirfield, All Saints Binfield in Berkshire, St Andrew's Backwell in Somerset, St Mary's in Liverpool's West Derby, South Cerney Church in Gloucestershire and All Saints Fulham where bells ring out as well.

Cambridge
At St John's College sixteen choristers and fourteen choral students of the College Choir sing from the top of the 163 foot high chapel tower at noon. As soon as the clock has struck 12 the service begins. The singing of a motet, two collects, an anthem and a hymn takes about eight minutes. Although the choir can be heard from the ground, amplification has recently been used which means that the singing is audible as far along the street as Heffers bookshop. However, in 2011, when Ascension Day was during the choristers' half-term holiday, the choral students sang without loudspeakers and were still clearly heard in First Court. The first St John's tower top singing in 1902 took place at noon without notice as a test to see if the music could be heard below. Some months earlier Dr Cyril Rootham, organist and Master of the Chapel Choir, had been involved in a discussion at High Table about the possibility of voices being heard from a

height. He suggested that they would be heard alright from the top of the tower but his two colleagues, biologist William Bateson and physicist Sir Joseph Larmor thought not. It was already the custom for choirboys to have an Ascension Day treat by going up the tower after morning service so he asked them to sing the motet. To his joy he noticed people below stop to listen and Larmor opened his window and look out. The Festal Eucharist precedes the tower singing.

At Great St Mary's singing takes place at 7.45am from the tower. At Christ's College motets are sung from the Great Gate at 8.30am.

Warwick

At 7am choirs in Warwick sing in succession from the tower of St Mary's Church and Lord Leycester Hospital chapel steps. The Boys' and Men's Voices at St Mary's sing an anthem, psalm and a hymn and the gospel is read. The Girl's Voices are at the hospital. The first tower top singing here was held at St Mary's in 1907. When the wind is in the right direction the choirs can be heard by the St Nicholas Church choir as it sings simultaneously from Warwick Castle's fourteenth-century Guy's Tower.

Lichfield

At 7.40am Lichfield Cathedral's senior choir boys sing two hymns, *The head that once was crowned* and *Hail the day that sees him rise*, from the top of the cathedral tower but standing inside the base of the hollow spire which acts as a loudspeaker. The sound is enhanced by two or three clarinets.

After a Liturgy of the Word service new lime branches are distributed to the congregation as it leaves the cathedral to begin a circuit of the close. The first station is at Eastgate where there is a reading, a prayer and a hymn. Music stands are draped in greenery and a sprig of lime is stuffed into letter boxes of houses passed on the perambulation. There are four more stops before the station outside the west end. At the words from Revelation 'Then God's temple in heaven was opened' the west doors swing open. The final stop is at the font where there is a renewal of baptismal promises before the priest blesses the crowd with water using a lime branch. Afterwards the lime branches are thrown into the font. The event takes about an hour and ends with the Eucharist at the high altar.

Oxford

Morning Prayer is sung an the top of Exeter College tower at 8am and the roof of Keble College chapel fifteen minutes later with the sound heard in Turle Street and then Blackhall Road. Merton College has an anthem and three hymns sung from the chapel tower at noon (having already been up the tower at 6pm yesterday). The final high rise musical performance is at Lincoln College where madrigals can be heard from the gatehouse almost twelve hours since Exeter College began in the same street.

Recently New College has started a tradition of climbing The Mound in the Fellows' Gardens to sing an anthem after the Sung Eucharist in the evening.

London

Somerset House in London has no tower but there is singing of Ascension Day hymns by King's College London chapel choir under the modern college entrance portico as commuters pass along The Strand. Outdoor singing is at 9.15am before the Eucharist. This tradition is only interrupted when the day coincides with examinations.

There is lunchtime singing at St Michael's Cornhill in the City where since 1987 the choir has climbed the tower to sing a hymn which can be heard in the enclosed churchyard.

Wells

Bisley

Dressing the Wells in this hilltop village of Bisley in Gloucestershire was begun in 1863 by rector Thomas Keble, brother of John. The Wells was restored that year at the instigation of Thomas to celebrate the wedding of the Prince of Wales. After a service in church, a band leads Bisley Blue Coat Primary School downhill to the Wells. Children at the front carry floral stars and large letters and numbers to spell the words 'ASCENSION DAY' and the year. Others carry posies to decorate the Wells. A prayer, song, blessing and hymn are followed by tea.

Tissington
At Tissington in Derbyshire, six wells are dressed ready for today (Hall, Hands, Coffin, Town, Yew Tree Wells and Children's). The custom started at least by 1349 when the pure water supply which never dries up may have saved the village from the Black Death. There is a 1758 record of the incumbent 'annually ... with his parishioners praying and singing' over the springs decorated with garlands on Ascension Day. Later that century the skill of making huge pictures with petals was introduced. New biblical scenes are created each year. The work started last Monday with 8 foot-high frames soaked in a pond before being filled with salted clay which had been subject to puddling (or treading). The outline is made with seeds and the colours depend on flowers available – an early date means plenty of bluebells. The petals are laid from the bottom like tiles with work going on late into the night. Once in place, the cover is not removed until midnight. After the 11am church service, the clergy and choir set out in procession to visit each well which, after a hymn and a psalm has been sung, is blessed. The decorations remain until 5pm next Wednesday evening.

Beating the Bounds
London
A procession, including the alderman of the Ward of Tower, common councillors, masters of livery companies, the bargemaster of the Company of Watermen and Lightermen accompanied by Doggett's Coat and Badge winners and twelve students of St Dunstan's College at Catford (which until 1888 was in the parish), set out at 4pm from All Hallows-by-the-Tower to beat

the bounds of the parish. This includes St Dunstan-in-the-East where the school was founded. Until the late 1940s when pupils just beat the bounds of St Dunstan's they had herbs tied to their sticks. As then the party also takes to a boat to reach the southern boundary in the middle of the Thames. After a lapse, annual beating the bounds was restored in 1978. Evensong follows at 6pm.

Every third year (2020/2023/2026) the All Hallows congregation stays on for a ceremonial confrontation with those beating the bounds of the Tower of London's Liberty. The liberty's extent was determined by the maximum reach of an arrow shot from the Tower. The first confrontation about the boundary between the parish and Tower took place on Ascension Day 1698 when, vestry minutes record, 'several warders of the Tower violently set upon' a churchwarden.

The first record of the ceremony is 1555 and a James II charter granted in 1687 confirming the Liberty boundary hangs in constable's office. Until as recently as 1975 the event was in the morning after an 11am service at St Peter-ad-Vincula. The procession of choir and Tower children emerges from the Tower led by the chief yeoman warder and chaplain accompanied by the governor and followed by Beefeaters. A bareheaded Beefeater carries the cross. At each of the thirty-one boundary stones (one is in an hotel foyer) there is a halt for the chaplain to shout: 'Cursed is he who moveth his neighbour's landmark' (Deuteronomy 27.17). The chief warder then gives the order to the children: 'Whack it, whack it!' The marker is hit with sticks – these were once willow wands more than twice the height of the child. After circling the Tower clockwise for about thirty minutes, the party reaches the Wharf where it enters Henry III's Watergate to end by singing the National Anthem outside the chapel.

St Botolph Aldgate beats the bounds at the end of the school day with a colourful procession including Sir John Cass Primary School pupils, the ward constable, beadle and clergy.

Oxford

The University Church beats the parish boundary after the 8.30am Eucharist. A 1714 Act of Parliament allows for the Ascension Day procession to pass through a doorway in Catte Street leading to All Souls College where breakfast for the participants includes cherry cake as a reminder that the college is partly built on a cherry orchard owned by the parish. Brasenose, University and Oriel Colleges are also visited.

After 9am Sung Eucharist at St Michael at the North Gate, the congregation and choir walk in procession with long sticks around the parish boundary. At each of twenty-nine boundary stones the rector chalks a cross and adds the date before the mark is beaten. The route is through Marks & Spencer where there is a brass cross in the floor; Zara, which has the oldest stone; Wagamama (once The Roebuck), Monsoon and St Peter's and Brasenose Colleges. A stone in the Old Bodleian Library wall is found already marked by the University Church which shares the boundary. By noon a stone is beaten in the Front Quad of Lincoln College which has been the church's patron since 1427, the year before beating the bounds started. Lunch served in the Hall includes ivy beer home brewed for today. A door connecting with Brasenose is opened for neighbouring students to enjoy the free beer tainted with ground ivy to discourage excessive drinking. Afterwards 3000 (once hot) pennies are thrown from the gatehouse roof into Front Quad where children scramble on the grass for the coins.

Portland, Dorset

A Beating the Bound ceremony lasting about fifteen minutes takes place every seven years (2023/2030) at the Bound Stone on Chesil Beach. A new stone replaced the old (but still standing) stone in 1995 on the westward Portland boundary on Chesil Beach which has water on both sides. Most of the sixty or seventy strong crowd witnessing the event arrive by barges from the nearby army base across the Fleet. At 10.30am the Crown local bailiff of the Island and Royal Manor of Portland welcomes everyone and the rector of Portland says a prayer. Next a surveyor, who has brought equipment, confirms that the compass bearings of the stone on the high shingle beach are correct. The rector reads the Ascension Day collect and a churchwarden reads St Matthew's account of the Ascension. The head boy and head girl of the Royal Manor School are ceremoniously and simultaneously beaten on the stone by being touched with a stick. Finally a stonemason incises the year on the stone.

Gospel Tree Service
Wicken, Northamptonshire
A service in the village church at 10.30am is followed by the rector leading the congregation to the Gospel Elm where prayers are said and the Old Hundreth hymn *All people that on earth do dwell* sung. Afterwards 'cakes and ale' are served in the Old Rectory. The custom began on Ascension Day 1587 when the parishes of Wyke-Hamon and Wyke-Dive were united as the one parish of Wicken and the rector provided cakes and ale to celebrate. The cake is a dark, soft fruit bread baked to a special recipe. St John's Church has survived whilst nearby St James' was demolished in 1619. The Gospel Elm was replaced in 1985 with a new tree. The stump of the old tree was dug up in 2000 but after protest by 98-year-old Gladys Eden, who lived opposite, the wood was returned. Early in the twentieth century the village children still wore special dresses for the Ascension Day ceremonies.

Seventh Sunday of Easter

What Happened This Week

Acts 1.15-26

After the Ascension there was just over a week before Pentecost during which the Apostles filled the vacancy among the Twelve caused by the defection on Maundy Thursday (see page 72) of Judas. Matthias won the ballot. (See St Matthias Day, page 202).

In Church

It is still the Easter season. Every third year (2018, 2021/2024) the story of Matthias' election is read at Mass.

Saturday Before Pentecost Sunday

In Church

The vigil Mass gospel (John 7.37-39) tells of Jesus during his ministry looking forward to the coming of the Spirit.

This evening's Mass can be part of a vigil of prayer and four readings following maybe evening prayer when the hymn *Come, Holy Ghost, our souls inspire* (Veni Creator Spiritus, c. 820) is sung.

Vestments are red.

Pentecost Sunday
Whitsun

Pentecost, the end of the fifty day Easter season, is the third great feast of the Church's year after Christmas and Easter. Christians recall the infant Church gathered with Mary under the leadership of Peter in the upper room in Jerusalem when the Holy Spirit dramatically descended in the form of fire and the sound of wind.

St John XXIII, as Pope, chose Pentecost 1960 to found the Secretariat (now Pontifical Council) for Promoting Christian Unity. He said that it was from the spirit and doctrine of Pentecost that the Vatican Council took 'its substance and its life'.

Whitsun

The old and now not so familiar name for Pentecost in Britain was *Whitsun* which is derived from the *white robes* worn at this time by newly baptised. Until the twelfth century christenings only took place at Easter and Pentecost. Whit was also the common name in Scandinavia but France has always had the more appropriate word Pentecôte for this feast.

The first event held in Westminster Hall was William II's 1099 Whitsun Feast. Parliament's fixed half-term break starting at the Spring Bank Holiday is still known as the Whitsun Recess. Until 1547 Whitsun was celebrated in St Paul's Cathedral by the swinging of a huge thurible from the ceiling, like Santiago's *botafumeiro*, and the release of doves representing the Holy Spirit. Sometimes in England it was arranged for burning filaments to rain down. But in in Italy red rose petals were dropped from church ceilings as still happens at the Pantheon in Rome (see page 144).

Philip Larkin's poem *The Whitsun Weddings* is a reminder of how the weekend was a shared holiday for most people. Moving Whit Monday Bank Holiday (see below) and the recent change of name from Whitsun to Pentecost has led to a loss in Britain of public awareness of this landmark in the Christian year.

What Happened Today
Acts 2.1-42
The Apostles, Jesus' mother, Mary and some cousins were waiting in a house where the Last Supper took place on Maundy Thursday (see page 69) in Jerusalem as they had been commanded on Ascension Day (see page 127). It was early morning and suddenly they heard a sound like a strong wind and saw tongues of fire rest on each other's head.

The disciples knew Pentecost as Jewish harvest festival celebrated fifty days after the Passover and originally marking Moses receiving the Ten Commandments on Mount Sinai. The appearance of fire and wind is reminiscent of God descending on that occasion 'in the form of fire' (Exodus 19.18). They would also have been aware of God's words in Joel 3, 'shall I pour out my spirit', with a reference to their own location, Mount Zion, in Jerusalem.

The disciples began to speak in foreign languages and the hubbub attracted passers-by, many Pentecost visitors from such far off places as Arabia, Libya, Crete and Rome, who were astonished to hear Galileans speaking in their own language. Others dismissed it all as drunken babbling but Peter addressed the crowd and by the end of the day about 3000 people had been baptised.

This was confirmation of Christ's words on Easter Day when he appeared to the Apostles in the evening saying 'Receive the Holy Spirit' (John 20.19-23; see page 101). It was also the beginning of today's Church made up of men and women of many races and cultures crossing frontiers.

In Church

Red vestments are worn today to represent the tongues of fire. In some places, especially New York, people often wear red hats, scarves or ties. The Mass begins with the congregation being sprinkled with holy water.

The first reading (Acts 2.1-11) tells what happened on the Church's first Pentecost.

Today is the last day for adding the Alleluia! exclamation after the blessing and the last day for the Easter candle to be lit in the sanctuary. After today it stands by the font for baptismal candles to be lit from as at the Easter Vigil or lit alongside a coffin to indicate that the death of a baptised person is a sharing in Christ's victory over death.

Hymns for today are *Come, Holy Ghost, our souls inspire*; *Come down, O love divine*; *Come thou Holy Spirit, come* and *O thou who camest from above*.

Also suitable is *Onward! Christian soldiers* which curate Sabine Baring-Gould wrote in ten minutes for the 1865 Whit Tuesday Walk at Horbury Bridge near Wakefield when children from St John's, led by the crucifer, walked over a mile up Quarry Hill to St Peter's. He set it to the slow movement of Haydn's Symphony in D, No. 15 but Sir Arthur Sullivan's 1871 tune, first heard at Child Okeford church in Dorset, has proved more popular.

Although this is the 'birthday' of the Church, when the main Mass is a big joyful musical occasion, it is appropriate to attend an 8am or 9am said Mass today for we know from Paul's speech that the incident took place before 9am.

Today Christians renew themselves for the rest of the year when they attempt to be witnesses and missioners, mainly by example, for their faith. This was the task entrusted to the Apostles by Christ just before the Ascension: 'Go … make disciples of all nations … and teach them to observe all the commands I gave you' (Matthew 28.19-20).

PENTECOST TRADITIONS

Whit Walks

In the nineteenth century, northern England saw popular street parades known as Whit Walks inspired by the account of the Apostles going into the streets of Jerusalem and parading their faith in many languages. The tradition started in 1801 with a walk between Manchester's St Ann's Church and the cathedral. There was huge rivalry between the Anglican congregations walking behind their parish banners on Whit Monday. From 1844 Manchester's Roman Catholic parishes walked together on Whit Friday. Girls wore new long white dresses and carried flowers or held the banners' ribbons whilst boys were in best suits. Often a brass band took part. Within living memory a walker from St Ann's recalled 'feeling proud to show others my belief'.

The Walks survive in the Manchester area now as ecumenical occasions with the main city walk from the cathedral to Albert Square and back on Spring Bank Holiday Monday. Parishes bring banners, robed choirs, processional crosses and there are several bands. Whit walks have seen a revival and numbers taking part rising since the Millennium. The Audenshaw walk involves three churches and ends with a service outside the Pack Horse; the Littleborough procession starts this afternoon at St Andrew's, Dearnley and finishes at Hare Hill Park; Newton's procession, begun in 2006, goes from Flowery Fields to Hyde Park. Barnsley restored its walk in 2014. There are also walks at Dukinfield, Royton, Stalybridge and Thornham.

West Yorkshire walks still take place on Whit Friday (see page 149).

In France the Paris-Chartres Pilgrimage is a three-day sixty-five mile Pentecost walk starting at 6am from Notre-Dame de Paris and reaching Chartres today. At least 8000 mainly young traditionalist pilgrims walk in 'chapters' of around twenty to fifty with a chaplain. This custom, revived in 1983, dates from the twelfth century.

Rush and Grass Strewing
Bristol
Today is known as Rush Sunday at St Mary Redcliffe where the floor of the church is covered with fresh-smelling green rushes and herbs. In 1493 provision was made by the lord mayor William Spencer for sermons before the lord mayor and Corporation on Whit Monday, Tuesday and Wednesday. Now there is just one sermon at a choral matins today when the lord mayor arrives by horse-drawn coach. In church he is preceded by the sword bearer and posies are carried as a 'protection against infection'.

Shenington, Oxfordshire
Grass from the Holy Trinity churchyard is strewn on the church floor on Pentecost Eve and renewed on the following two Saturdays. There is a distinctive smell until the grass is finally cleared on the Saturday after Corpus Christi. The custom, once widespread at Pentecost and especially in the Salisbury Diocese, was first recorded here in 1720. In medieval times rushes were often used to carpet a church floor on special occasions. In winter it covered cold stone and in hot summer weather the smell would mask unpleasant odours.

Whitsun Cakes
Preston, Lancashire
Goosnargh Cakes are traditional Whitsun cakes eaten in the Preston area. Goosnargh (pronounced 'goosner') cakes are very thick biscuits with caraway seeds and sometimes covered in caster sugar, once sold in thousands as a Whitsun treat having originated at the nearby Goosnargh where around 50,000 were sold for a penny each during the village Whit Walk. They are now made by Tina's Corner Bakery in nearby Longridge and delivered to Goosnargh Post Office. In 2013 the cakes were recognised as a Forgotten Food worth saving by Slow Food UK. A Whitsuntide Festival, a successor to its Whit walk, is held in Goosnargh on the Saturday following Spring Bank Holiday. Preston's Whit Fair in the Flag Market is now on Spring Bank Holiday Monday.

Bread and Cheese Throwing

St Briavel's, Forest of Dean, Gloucestershire

Pentecost is marked at St Briavel's (pronounced 'Brevel's') with England's oldest unbroken custom. This begins at St Mary's Church at 7pm evensong when the Whittington Purse sermon is preached outside. The Whittington family made provision for the preacher to be paid £6/8d. During the service two baskets of diced bread and cheese are blessed. Afterwards the clergy and choir stand on the roof to throw the bread and cheese to a waiting crowd between the church and the castle. One basket is held by the Keeper of the Wood. Cubs once held out their caps to catch the food but now inverted umbrellas are sometimes used. The distribution takes fifteen minutes, leaving the road covered in trodden bread and cheese.

The custom started about 1130 when food was distributed to the poor after the Whitsun Mass. Later bread and cheese was thrown from the gallery in the church but rowdy scenes, involving hard cheese being thrown at the vicar in the pulpit, caused the throwers to be moved outside to the top of the tower from about 1857. Since the custom is said to preserve the right of villagers to collect wood from nearby Hudnall's Wood it is keenly maintained.

Petal Shower

Rome

Today is known *Pasqua Rossa* meaning *Red Easter*. At the end of Solemn Mass at the Pantheon petals shower down from the dome as the choir sings *Veni, Creator Spiritus*.

Whit Monday

Pre-Reformation there were parish parties called Whitsun Ales which involved drinking celebratory brews and Morris dancing. Shakespeare mentions 'a Whitsun morris-dance' in *Henry V*. The Chipping Camden Olimpics, still held around this time, was founded in 1612 as a Whit Week event. Whit Monday was long taken as a holiday. The Old Vic Theatre advertised its grand opening on 'Whit Monday 1818'. In 1851 the White Bear Tavern, near London's Kennington Common, staged an afternoon of 'rustic and athletic games' featuring such fun as a jingling match and a sack race.

The 1871 Bank Holidays Act made the nationwide custom of taking the day off on Monday official and continued to keep Pentecost as a major landmark in the year until 1965 when the holiday was fixed in the UK on the last Monday in May and renamed Spring Bank Holiday. The Irish Republic moved the holiday to the first Monday in June. Many Whitsun fairs and customs are now held on the new Spring Bank Holiday or another date. Thaxted in Essex has moved its famous Whitsun Morris dancing, revived in 1911, to the first weekend in June.

Whit Monday, which can fall on a date between 11 May and 14 June, occasionally will coincide with the fixed holiday date as in 2020, 2023, 2034 and 2039. So if today is also the Spring Bank Holiday there is Morris dancing at Bampton and Headington in Oxfordshire; the Anglican National Pilgrimage to the Shrine of Our Lady at Walsingham and cheese rolling on Cooper's Hill in Gloucestershire. The St Martin-in-the Fields four-day walk from Trafalgar Square to Canterbury, a tradition since 1990, reaches the cathedral today.

The Pinner Fair held in the High Street on the Wednesday

after the Spring Holiday was originally a Whit Wednesday event started in 1336.

The Bahamas still has a 'Whit Monday Holiday' and today remains a holiday in Germany. Recent attempts by the French government to make today a normal working day met with such strong resistance, including mass absenteeism, that the *Lundi de Pentecôte* holiday has been restored.

In Church

From today and for the rest of year, apart from special occasions, the vestments colour is green for growth.

Whit Monday Customs on Spring Bank Holiday

Coopers Hill near Birdlip, Gloucestershire

As many as 15,000 people assemble on Cooper's Hill to watch cheese rolling at 12 noon. The ancient custom ensured the villagers' rights to graze sheep on the hill and has long taken place at Whitsun. The four races (one women's) start at the summit which is marked by a maypole topped by a cockerel. On a count of three the cheese is rolled and on four the maybe twenty competitors chase the 7lb Double Gloucester for 200 yards down the hill. The first person to arrive at the bottom wins the cheese which is made at Old Ley Court farm at nearby Birdwood. Seven wheels of cheese are needed. The event was cancelled due to the foot and mouth crisis in 2001 and again two years later when the first aid team was diverted to Algeria for an earthquake. Injuries on the very steep hill can be high. In 2012 foam was substituted for the cheese after police warned the 86-year-old cheesemaker that she may be liable for any injuries. In 2014 a Dutch cheesemaker offered Gouda cheeses but the use of local cheese was reinstated.

Manchester

The city's main Whit Walk involving around 1500 people in the morning is open to all and over two hours makes its way from the cathedral to Albert Square for a short service and back.

Walsingham, Norfolk
The annual Anglican National Pilgrimage, first held on Whit
Monday 1938, attracts parish parties for a street procession and
Mass in the abbey ruins.

Whit Tuesday

The Dancing Procession

The Dancing Procession at Echternach in Luxembourg is held in honour of St Willibrord of York who was born in Yorkshire in 658, educated at Ripon and became the first Bishop of Utrecht. There he worked with Devon-born St Boniface. After a missionary life in Germany and Holland he moved to Echternach where he founded the abbey and died in 739.

All morning around 12,000 dancers in forty-five groups form a procession, five abreast, to dance, two steps forward one step back, through the streets and into the abbey crypt to pass Willibrord's tomb. Bishops lead the procession with the dance rhythm, a folk tune melody, played in turn by musical societies. The origin of this custom, first mentioned in 1497, may be the paying of tithes to the abbey due at Pentecost.

St Willibrord is patron saint of Luxembourg and Holland where he is a focus for ecumenical activity. In Britain the St Willibrord Society, having helped establish full communion in 1931 between Anglicans and Old Catholic Churches of the Union of Utrecht, promotes Anglican-Old Catholic links.

Whit Friday

Yorkshire Whit Walks

Charlotte Brontë, in her novel *Shirley* written in 1848, described Whit walks in West Yorkshire as 'a joyous scene, and a scene to do good'. The custom remains strong with today being a local holiday as shops display 'closed for Whit Friday' notices.

Saddleworth church congregations and Sunday schools held Whit walks on different days in Whit week until the 1850s when they were amalgamated on Friday. However, although from at least 1887 there was often a joint outdoor singing of hymns, churches still maintained separate walks led by its own brass band. In 1920 Anglicans and Methodists in Greenfield combined to walk round the village with the vicar of St Mary's claiming that this was to be in the spirit of Pentecost and not just to save money on having to hire several bands. Now all walks are ecumenical occasions.

A Churches Together banner leads the walk from Top Mossley with robed clergy, servers with incense and statues, Scouts and Brownies. At 10am there a recitation of the Lord's Prayer and the Grace interspersed by the singing of *Jerusalem*, before the two-hour walk to Bottom Mossley and back.

During the late afternoon and evening, in a tradition begun at Uppermill and dating from 1884, the villages host outdoor brass band contests involving as many as a hundred and thirty-five bands. Black Dyke Brass Band has played since the 1888 Mossley walk. In Uppermill bands march one by one along the closed main road and round to the back of the library to perform their chosen piece. In Mossley bands go along the side of the market square. The adjudicator sits inside a building so as not to see the band or know its name. Such is the enthusiasm that the contests tend to last until well after 10pm.

TRINITY

TRINITY SUNDAY

The Trinity is God the Father, Son and Holy Spirit. This is the same as God, Jesus and the spirit of Pentecost – the three in one.

The Trinity

It is as the Holy Trinity that God reaches out through his son and the Holy Spirit. According to the Roman Catholic Catechism 'The mystery of the Most Holy Trinity is the central mystery of the Christian faith and life ... It is the most fundamental and essential teaching'.

It is in the name of the Father, Son and Holy Spirit that we become members of the Church and gather together at least Sunday by Sunday.

Theophilus of Antioch, a second-century bishop, was the first person to speak of the Triad or Trinity of God.

Trinity Sunday

Trinity Sunday was first celebrated by Bishop Stephen of Liège in the early tenth century and by the twelfth century the custom had spread to France where it was observed at Cluny Abbey. Archbishop Thomas Becket introduced it to England having been consecrated and enthroned as Archbishop at Canterbury Cathedral on the Sunday after Pentecost (or Trinity Sunday) 1162. Appropriately his shrine was placed in the Trinity Chapel. Two centuries later in 1334 Pope John XXII, who added this week's Corpus Christi (see page 157) which also originated in Liége, included Trinity Sunday in the universal calendar.

Trinity week was once marked by annual outdoor fairs such as the one in Christchurch, on the Hampshire border, where the priory is dedicated to the Trinity. In 1215 the barons chose Trinity week as a significant time for King John to formally give his assent to Magna Carta.

Today marks the start of the second half of the year which runs to Advent. This week's Corpus Christi is an extra feast to complete the Maundy Thursday celebration. Otherwise the ordinary Sundays to come are a time for growth in Christ as we hear in the weekly readings the story of God as Christ coming among us. His final words at the Ascension (see page 128) and God's gift at Pentecost (page 139) are reminders that, having lived out the events of Holy Week and the resurrection appearances, Christians are to grow in faith and to spread the faith.

In Church

Today's vestments are white but from tomorrow, and on the following Sundays in ordinary time, the colour returns to green, representing growth. Next Thursday there will be a brief return to white for Corpus Christi (see page 157) but green will become familiar until Advent as will the pascal candle being by the font.

The hymn *Holy, holy, holy*, which includes the line 'God in three Persons, blessed Trinity', was written for today around 1815 by Reginald Heber, vicar of Hodnet in Shropshire who became Bishop of Calcutta. *I bind unto myself today*, known as 'St Patrick's Breastplate' and sung on St Patrick's Day, is also a Trinity hymn. The oldest is *All hail, adored Trinity* which is adapted from a tenth-century hymn *Ave colenda Trinitas*.

Trinity Customs
Kirtlington, Oxfordshire
The Lamb Ale feast, once held on Trinity Monday, is the last survivor of those held in many places including nearby Kidlington and Eynsham to celebrate Whitsun and Trinity. The involvement of Morris dancing dates from at least 1679 when Thomas Blount saw 'a Morisco dance of Men' and the 'rest of the day ... spent in dancing, mirth and jollity'. At Whitsun 1732 there is a record

of the lord of the manor Sir George Dashwood paying 'Kertling Morris' five shillings. In advance a live lamb was carried round the village as part of a fund-raising effort.

Kirtlington's Lamb Ale, officially abandoned in 1858, was revived by Kirtlington Morris in 1979. On Trinity Eve there is now an evening Lamb Roast and Barn Dance in theVillage Hall attended by visitors who camp behind the church.

Today at 10am a long outdoor procession of around fourteen Morris sides makes its way through the village to the church for the Lamb Ale Service which includes dancing. Afterwards there is a procession to the school where real ale and refreshments are available. During the afternoon a fun fair opens on the green and there is more dancing outside The Dashwood Arms and The Oxford Arms.

The Lamb Ale is held back a week when Trinity coincides with the Spring Bank Holiday.

Rothwell, Northamptonshire

Councillors and clergy walk in procession from a civic service at Holy Trinity Church to Market Hill where at 3pm there is the blessing of the Rowell Fair. This evolved from a horse fair, still viable in the 1920s, into a fun fair. A charter, granted in 1204 by King John at Westminster, and witnessed by the Archbishop of Canterbury and the Bishops of London and Norwich, confirmed 'a fair at Rowell (Rothwell) at the feast of the Holy Trinity for and during the five days'.

On Trinity Monday, when the church clock has struck 6am, the lord of the manor's bailiff, mounted on horseback outside the west door, reads a 1614 charter to a crowd of around 2000 people. This is followed by a brass band playing the national anthem. Afterwards the procession, accompanied by halberdiers, moves to the war memorial where the band plays psalm 23.

From now on the crowd becomes slightly noisy as the charter reading and national anthem is repeated outside eight pubs or former pubs around the town. After each ceremony the pub gives the bailiff a rum and milk whilst the halberdiers receive beer. At each stop local youths are allowed to attempt disarming the halberdiers for a few moments until a police officer blows a whistle. The final pub visited is the Charter Inn at about 7.15am.

Traditional local Trinity fare is boiled ham and Rothwell Tart.

Southwold, Suffolk
The Trinity Fair is held for three days usually from Trinity Monday although recently it has opened just before the weekend. The mayor, who opens the fair, walks in procession with councillors around the South Green fairground before riding on an attraction. Afterwards the town clerk reads the Fair Charter which he repeats in the Market Place.

Corpus Christi
Thursday after Trinity Sunday

Corpus Christi meaning *Body of Christ* is a feast of celebration and thanksgiving for the institution of the Holy Communion. It is on a Thursday to recall Maundy Thursday.

Today thanks can be given more joyfully than was possible on Maundy Thursday (see page 69) when the first Eucharist was commemorated. On that night congregations were in the midst of Holy Week and, although the bells were rung for joy at the Gloria, all knew that commemoration of Christ's arrest, torture, trial and death were to follow almost immediately. On Maundy Thursday there is also an emphasis on loving one another and Christ's humble act of washing feet. Now, having celebrated the resurrection (see page 99), Ascension (see page 127) and Pentecost (see page 139), thanks can be given with greater happiness and confidence.

'They do it in colossal cathedrals, on kitchen tables, in chapels built on the cheap, at Baroque altars in which an instant of religious drama has been frozen in stone and contrived light, in rooms over public houses that still smell of beer and occasionally, still, in upper rooms with the doors guarded,' wrote Patrick O'Donovan in 1967 when attempting to explain the significance of the Eucharist. 'A man bends over a piece of unleavened bread and over a silver gilt cup with a little wine and water in it and he pronounces a formula more terrible than the sound of guns … And the majority of Christians believe that God himself is immediate and present, not in the way that he is everywhere anyway, but in the way that a man is there in the same room.'

Christ is believed to be truly present in the bread and wine which becomes not physically but sacramentally the body and blood of Christ. It is both a thanksgiving to God and a sacred meal which nourishes spiritually each week.

The Eucharist is the summit and source of Christian living according to the Second Vatican Council. Pope John Paul II, in a letter signed in the Upper Room during his Holy Land pilgrimage, said: 'The mystery of the Eucharist, which proclaims and celebrates the Death and Resurrection of Christ until he comes again, is the heart of the Church's life.'

Development of the Feast

The Corpus Christi feast originated at Liège in Belgium after lobbying by Augustinian nun St Juliana of Liège (1192-1258) who came to see herself, as Jesus' mother Mary, a 'handmaid of the Lord'. From the age of 16 Juliana began having dreams about an imperfect moon and claimed to have seen Christ explaining that the missing wedge of moon was a missing feast in the Christian year which should be dedicated to the Eucharist. Twenty years later Juliana, by then prioress of Mont Cornillon, confided in John of Lausanne, canon of the city's hilltop collegiate church of St Martin. Juliana sometimes stayed there in the guest room of her friend Blessed Eve. John and Eve were Juliana's greatest supporters in her bid to have the new feast recognised. Words for the Mass and vespers were devised by Juliana and John.

A decade later Canon John spoke to a new Bishop of Liège Robert Torote who proved sympathetic and in 1242 visited Juliana. Corpus Christi Mass was first celebrated in St Martin's on Thursday 14 June 1246, 'the Thursday after the octave of the Trinity' when the bishop ordered the inclusion of the feast in the diocesan calendar.

Unfortunately Bishop Torote died in October and his successor, Henry proved less enthusiastic and even supported Juliana's removal as prioress. However, in 1251 Hugh of St Cher, a Dominican and the new cardinal-legate to Germany, visited Liège and kept the festival at St Martin's. He decreed that the date should be the 'Thursday after the octave of Pentecost' rather than the octave of Trinity and this date has been retained.

In 1258 exiled Juliana died at Fosses-La-Ville. Three years later the former archdeacon of the Liège, Jacques Pantaleon became Pope Urban IV. His summer residence was at Orvieto in Italy where in 1263 he was impressed by a miracle at nearby Bolsena. Blood dripped from consecrated bread on to a corporal at St Christina's Church as a doubting priest celebrated Mass. The cloth was taken at once to the Pope who declared the event to be a miracle. On 11 August of the following year he issued a Papal Bull proclaiming the feast of Corpus Christi to be part of the universal calendar. The Pope, who had known Juliana, may have been influenced by Hugh of St Cher who had died in 1246 whilst part of the Papal household at Orvieto. Thomas Aquinas, who was living there, re-wrote Juliana's liturgy. However, only a few letters informing dioceses of this news had been sent when the Pope died in October.

So at the end of the thirteenth century the feast was only being observed in a few places beyond Liège, such as Cologne, Laon, Venice, Toledo (where it remains a huge occasion) and Seville.

There were twelve more popes before 1317 when John XXII re-promulgated the Bull whilst in exile in Avignon. A letter announcing the new feast to the English Church was dated 3 January 1318 and reached London about 16 January. That year Corpus Christi was observed at Gloucester Abbey (now Cathedral). The Bath and Wells Diocese made arrangements for the following year and in 1322 the Archbishop of York ordered the day to be kept throughout his Northern Province.

Langland's *Piers Plowman* which was written about 1375 mentions the 'Copus Christi feste'. In 1393 the Skinners Company in the City of London started its annual Corpus Christi procession (see below) and in 1394 the Fraternity and Guild of Corpus Christi now known as the Salters' Company was formed. Lavenham in Suffolk has a magnificent guildhall built about 1530 by the town's Guild of Corpus Christi which was formed early in the previous century and organised the annual procession.

The Liège Diocese continued to use the original office texts co-written by Juliana, rather than the Aquinas version, until as late as 1509.

Corpus Christi Dedications

Corpus Christi College at Cambridge was founded in 1352 by the town Guilds of Corpus Christi and the Blessed Virgin Mary. Corpus Christi College at Oxford dates from 1517.

St Mary and Corpus Christi at Down Hatherley near Gloucester had the second dedication added when the church was rebuilt in the fifteenth century.

Corpus Christi Church in Covent Garden's Maiden Lane was, when opened in 1874, only the second English church to have the dedication. The windows above the high altar depict St Juliana and St Thomas Aquinas. Until 1974, when Covent Garden Flower Market moved, the church was lavishly decorated for the Corpus Christi festival with flowers.

Feast of Body and Blood

Since 1969 the official, although little used, feast day name has been *Corpus et Sanguis Christi* meaning the *Body and Blood of Christ*. This followed Pope Paul VI's decision to merge the Feast of The Precious Blood (1 July), which had been instituted in 1849 by Pius IX, with Corpus Christi.

The official change would probably meet with Juliana's approval as she wished people to be able to receive both the bread and the wine on the feast day.

Processions

The Solemnity of Corpus Christi consists of both the Mass and the procession afterwards when the consecrated bread, the body of Christ, is carried outdoors. Vatican II's Eucharistic Mysterium, published in 1967, confirmed the importance of the outdoor procession by which 'the Christian people give public witness to their faith and devotion towards this sacrament'.

The first recorded procession was in 1277 at St Gereon's in Cologne. The processional route in York saw bedspreads hung from windows and flowers and rushes scattered on the paving. The elaborate early nineteenth-century procession in Rome through the St Peter's Square colonnade was preceded by Vatican gardeners with baskets on their backs strewing myrtle.

The procession is, unlike the sombre procession on Maundy Thursday evening to the Garden of Gethsemane, a joyful walk with Christ and a response to his final call just before the Ascension for his message to go to the far corners of the world.

As early as 1419 Lincoln held its procession on the Sunday. The tradition of huge outdoor processions on the following Sunday in Cardiff and Manchester died out as the twentieth century closed. In 1981 20,000 were present in Manchester whilst 15,000 gathered in Cardiff Arms Park. By 1994 Cardiff attracted just 4000. But in this century there has been a revival of the street procession in Amsterdam, London and Limerick. In 2000 Oxford's procession, involving religious orders and parishes along St Giles, was revived after a gap of thirty-five years and has continued to attract hundreds each year.

Carpet of Flowers

Sometimes the procession sets out over a carpet of flowers either indoors or sometimes outdoors. Much community co-operation and love goes into creating a new design year by year. Arundel Cathedral is well-known for its floral carpet (see below). On the following Sunday evening St Mary's Bourne Street in Chelsea has an indoor herb carpet which gives off an aroma when crushed by feet as the elaborate Blessed Sacrament procession passes across it. At Camaiore in Italy, also on Sunday, the streets are given an illustrated sawdust carpet.

Mystery Plays

Several cities had trade guilds which staged a morality or biblical play performed on Corpus Christi. The York tradition, an all-day play beginning early in the morning with the Creation and ending with the Last Judgement near midnight, started within seventy years of the introduction of the feast. The processions and drama owed much to merchants who had witnessed the feast day in the Low Countries and they organised and sponsored the event.

In some places these annual performances continued after the Reformation upheavals as in Louth where it was staged in the market place until 1558. Chester's, seen by young William Shakespeare, was maintained until 1578, well into Elizabeth I's reign, by being branded as a Whitsun celebration.

The outdoor York Mystery Plays, revived for the 1951 Festival of Britain and now regularly staged, were known as the Corpus Christi Play. A 1463 text survives. A young Judi Dench had several roles and in 1957 played Mary alongside her father's Joseph. So powerful were the plays performed in Millennium Year that Archbishop David Hope said: 'People went out from the Mysteries to change their lives.'

Chester Mystery Plays, also revived for the Festival of Britain, are in June every fifth year (2018/2023) with a cast of more than two hundred. Coventry has an annual Mysteries Week arts festival at this time inspired by its mystery heritage.

In the Bible

Matthew 26.26-28; Mark 14.22-25; Luke 22.17-20; 1 Corinthians 11.23-26

The Eucharist was instituted at the Last Supper and at once became the weekly custom of the first Christians.

In Church

The preface (words before the sanctus in the Mass) recalls the Last Supper but sometimes the Maundy Thursday preface is repeated today.

Most celebrations involve carrying the Blessed Sacrament in procession. When there is no carpet it is the custom to scatter flower petals in the path of the priest carrying the sacrament, often under a splendid canopy. In ancient times it was usual to scatter flowers in the path of honoured guests and so it is done when Christ is with us in procession.

A popular hymn is *Of the glorious body telling* (Pange Lingua), written by Thomas Aquinas for today's Vespers, which includes the last two verses known from its opening words 'Therefore we before him bending' as the *Tantum Ergo*. Another is *Soul of my Saviour, sanctify my breast* (or *Anima Christi*) sung to a nineteenth-century tune although the words are believed to be a translation of the Latin prayer written by Pope John XXII. *Sweet sacrament divine*, which first appeared in 1858, is by Francis Stanfield who later became rector of Corpus Christi, Maiden Lane. The tune is by Charles Cox who was a curate at Our Lady of Victories in Kensington.

Today at Liège

The main Mass at St Martin's Church in Liège, the first church to celebrate the feast (see above), is in the evening with the bishop usually presiding. Afterwards there is a procession downhill to the cathedral. Elsewhere in Belgium the festival is observed on the following Sunday.

Corpus Christi Events

Arundel, Sussex

A carpet of flowers is laid in Arundel Cathedral for a Mass today. The custom dates back to 1877, four years after the opening of the church. The Duke of Norfolk, having seen the floral carpets in the streets of Sutri outside Rome, introduced one to Arundel. The tradition was broken during the World War I, when the Arundel Castle gardeners were unavailable, but revived in 1919 with parishioners undertaking the work. The 93-foot long carpet is laid by Tuesday evening and on view all day Wednesday and today. Mass is at 5.30pm followed by a procession over the carpet and down London Road to the castle for Benediction.

Cambridge

At Corpus Christi College, Cambridge today is a Scarlet Day in the calendar along with Christmas Day and Pentecost. A choral Eucharist at 5pm begins with a procession from St Catherine's College opposite. In the evening a procession from St Benet's to Little St Mary's passes the college.

London

Since 2004 the All Saints Margaret Street evening Solemn Mass is followed by a procession round the parish. The route includes part of Oxford Street where leaflets are given to onlookers to explain what is happening.

On Sunday afternoon there is a Procession from The Assumption Church in Warwick Street to Spanish Place in Marylebone. This custom began in 2014 and attracts about 2000 people.

The Skinners Company, founded in 1327 as the Fraternity of Corpus Christi, walks in procession at 2pm from Skinners Hall on the City of London's Dowgate Street to St James Garlickhythe. This procession, which ceased to include the Blessed Sacrament in about 1558, dates from 1393 when it was the City's most important Corpus Christi procession with about 200 clergy and the lord mayor taking part. The processional route went to St John Walbank until the Great Fire in 1666 destroyed the church and the service switched to St Antholin's which stood further west along Watling Street until demolished in 1875. At first the procession to St Antholin was at 7am. As late as 1830 girls would still accompany the procession to strew herbs as in the days when the Blessed Sacrament was present.

Oxford

Corpus Christi College has a Solemn Eucharist followed by dinner.

Cologne

Cologne Cathedral's main Mass is celebrated outdoors in the

square on the south side at 10am. This is followed by a procession with representatives of all the parishes, including St Gereon's which staged the first ever. The crowd genuflects as the Blessed Sacrament, preceded by a cloud of incense from four thuribles, is carried from the square. Several thousand people, including guilds, papal knights, ethnic and youth groups carrying flags, process through the two main squares and the shopping centre which is quiet as today is a public holiday.

Bolsena

On Sunday the first of five Masses in St Cristina's Church is celebrated at the altar of the miracle. In a custom held since 1811 carpets of flowers and a series of floral mats are laid along narrow streets leading to San Salvatore Church. At 6pm a procession sets out carrying the Blessed Sacrament and a blood-stained stone on an almost two-mile round journey.

Orvieto

A weekend of devotion and celebration starts on Friday. The streets are decorated with flowers for Sunday morning's procession when, after 9am Solemn Mass at the cathedral, the Blessed Sacrament and the Holy Corporal from Bolsena are carried together out of the cathedral. The long street procession with many banners, music and people in medieval costume has been held since 1338, the year after the 3 foot high corporal reliquary was made.

Andalusia

This morning in Zahara de la Sierra, a mountain village near Cadiz, there is a procession through streets turned green with fresh strewn grass on the ground and more grass and branches covering walls and buildings. This tradition dates from 1483.

Trinidad and Tobago

Today is a public holiday in Trinidad and Tobago where there is a tradition of both processions and the planting of seedlings.

SPECIAL DAYS WITH A FIXED DATE

St Valentine's Day

14 February

Today is St Cyril and St Methodius Day which takes precedence over the popular St Valentine who was dropped from the universal calendar in 1969.

St Cyril and St Methodius

Brothers Cyril and Methodius born in Thessalonica in 826 and 815, were pioneers of the vernacular. Both became priests and in 863 were invited to be missionaries in Moravia where they translated the New Testament and the liturgy into the Slavonic language. Good King Wenceslas' grandfather was converted by the two saints. The Cyrillic alphabet takes its name from Cyril who inspired it through his wish to see books written in Slavic. In 869 he became a monk but died a few days later on 14 February in Rome where he is buried in the Church of San Clemente. Methodius was Archbishop of Moravia and died in 885 at Velehrad in Czechoslovakia, where he was buried in a now lost cathedral. In 1980 Pope John Paul II made Cyril and Methodius patrons of Europe along with saints Benedict, Bridget of Sweden, Catherine of Sienna and Edith Stein. The Pope also moved the Cyril and Methodius feast day from 11 May.

St Valentine

St Valentine, Bishop of Terni in Italy, was martyred in Rome on 14 February 269 during persecution of Christians by Emperor Claudius II. It has been suggested that Valentine was beheaded for officiating at the weddings of soldiers against the wish of Claudius, who did not want troops distracted by lovers.

Valentine is buried in Terni on the Flaminian Way. Rome's Porto del Popolo, at the start of the Flaminian Way, was known as Porto del Valentino.

He is the patron of bee keepers, engaged couples, epilepsy, fainting, greetings, happy marriages, love, lovers, plague, travellers and young people. Several churches are dedicated to him, especially in America, including one in Bloomfield, New Jersey.

St Valentine's Day

Today has been St Valentine's Day since about 498 when Valentine was canonised by Pope Gelasius I allegedly to deflect attention from the Roman festival of Lupercalia when young men and women chose partners. This may have led to the day being associated with love. An old rhyme says:

> *Bachelors who'd married be*
> *Ere the Easter candles shine*
> *Make their prayer full lustily*
> *To the good St Valentine.*

But the first person to associate Valentine with romantic love was poet John Gower who died in 1408 at Southwark Priory (now Cathedral) where his effigy shows his head resting on his books. Gower's *Cinkante Balades* mentioning birds choosing mates today was echoed by his friend Geoffrey Chaucer in *The Parliament of Fowles*. Soon after Benedictine priest John Lydgate, who was influenced by Chaucer, wrote of 'Saynt Valentyne' and 'Cupydes Kalundere'. William Shakespeare, who knew Gower's work, repeats the bird-mating suggestion in *A Midsummer Night's Dream* and has Ophelia in *Hamlet* say: 'Tomorrow is Saint Valentine's day ... To be your Valentine.' John Donne, in his poem *Epithalamiom* written in 1613, includes the line 'Haile Bishop Valentine, whose day this is'. In the 1660s Samuel Pepys mentions 'Valentine's day' in his diary.

It has been suggested that the very first 'Valentine' was

a non-romantic letter signed 'your Valentine' by St Valentine when writing to a young girl who had been cured of blindness. Valentine cards developed out of letters and the earliest known card was sent in 1416 by Charles, Duke of Orleans from his cell in the Tower of London to his wife in France. The first sent within England was in 1477 by John Paston to 'my ryght welebeloved Voluntyne' Margery Brews. She concluded 'No more to you at this time, but the Holy Trinity have you in keeping' and signed with her initials in the form of a heart.

Scotland's oldest card, dated 1784, includes a long love poem and folds into a small box. Birmingham Library has one dated 1797. In 1825, when recipients still had to pay the postage, 13 February was the busiest night for the post office in London and by 1835 at least 60,000 were being sent. A century later Rex Whistler designed a St Valentine's Telegram sent by around 47,000 people.

Now the number of cards posted is second only to Christmas with a quarter of the United Kingdom population buying Valentine cards. Around £40m is spent on flowers.

Lover in Wiltshire had a surge of mail for hand franking on 13 February until 2008 when its tiny post office closed. Since 2017 the parish, which claims to be 'the most romantic village in the world', has opened an office every February where for a fee you can obtain a 'Posted at Lover' handstamp on envelopes prior to posting.

Another popular postmark is Valentine in Texas. The small town was founded when the Southern Pacific Railroad reached there on 14 February 1882 and the post office opened four years later.

St Valentine is seen in a mosaic in Jerusalem's Church of the Dormition. The Australian Roman Catholic bishops began a campaign in 2010 to reclaim the day as an occasion 'to promote and affirm marriage and life-long romantic love'.

In 2014 the Vatican's Pontifical Council for the Family recognised the enduring appeal of St Valentine by a holding a special event today in St Peter's Square for engaged couples.

Relics

Valentine's cranium is among his bones in the St Valentine Basilica at Terni in Italy which was built in 1618 after discovery of the decapitated body. On the eve of the Week of Prayer for Christian Unity in 2003 the Bishop of Terni presented the Russian Orthodox Patriarch with a relic.

Hyde Abbey in Winchester claimed to have Valentine's head (originally given by King Cnut's widow Emma to the cathedral) from its earliest days until dissolution in 1539. But today his alleged skull is displayed in Madrid, Kiedrich in Germany, St Valentino Torio near Pompei and Santa Maria in Cosmedin Rome. A section of the head is at the parish church of Chelmno in Poland.

The Basilica of St Peter and St Paul in Vyšehrad Castle in Prague, Czech Republic, has a shoulder blade probably brought to Prague in the fourteenth century by Holy Roman Emperor Charles IV. It was rediscovered in 2002 having been placed in storage during the nineteenth century when St Valentine had little popular appeal in Eastern Europe.

There is a Valentine bone in the Old St Ferdinand Shrine church at Florissant, Missouri in the USA where his replica figure lies under the altar. A small relic is displayed at Vico del Gargano in Italy's Puglia. A shard of bone from Valentine's finger is displayed annually at St John's Church in Coventry.

Fine chests containing alleged relics can be found in Birmingham, Dublin, Glasgow, Roquemaure in France, Vienna and Mytilini on the island of Lesbos in Greece. There is a possibility that the number of relics may be due to there having been at least two martyrs called Valentine, a priest and a bishop, dying on the same date although maybe not the same year. A second Valentine is thought to have been buried, like the first, on the Flaminian Way although nearer to Rome. Some Orthodox calendars include St Valentine priest and martyr on 6 July and St Valentine bishop and martyr on 30 July.

In Church

The collect is:

> *All powerful, ever living God,*
> *You gave St Valentine the courage to witness to the Gospel*
>   *of Christ,*
> *even to the point of giving his life for it.*
> *By his prayers help us to endure all suffering for love of you*
> *and to seek you with all our hearts,*
> *for you alone are the source of life.*
> *Grant this through our Lord Jesus Christ. Amen.*

Mass readings are James 1.2-4, 12 and John 12.24-26. Prayers are said for those in love and involved in relationships and marriage.

Anglican *Common Worship* includes A Service for St Valentine's Day.

Today at St Valentine's Tomb

In Terni, which has a statue of the saint, the Valentine relics are in a glass-fronted coffin below an altar in the Basilica of St Valentine. Today there are eight masses from 6am to 7pm including a Solemn Pontifical Mass this morning. The day ends with fireworks outside the church. Since 1989 this is just part of the city's almost month-long celebration which includes an award given for an act of love beyond others (recipients include Israeli premier Yitzhak Rabin) and a Celebration of Promise Mass for engaged couples who receive a certificate. Outdoor vendors sell, in aid of charity, red flowers for couples to place in the church. This gesture is in keeping with the tradition that Valentine picked fresh flowers from his garden to give to young visitors.

St Valentine Events

Birmingham

An altar in Birmingham Oratory contains a visible large casket with the remains of Valentine given by Pope Pius IX to John Henry Newman when he was leaving Rome in 1847 to found the Congregation of the Oratory. His coat of arms, devised when he became a cardinal, includes three hearts representing the Trinity. The motto 'Heart speaks unto heart' became the official slogan for Pope Benedict's visit to the UK in 2010. The Oratory, by agreement with Pius IX, still has its St Valentine Mass a week late on Newman's birthday 21 February.

Dublin

Relics of St Valentine in a wooden box, sent by Pope Gregory XVI, arrived in 1836 at Our Lady of Mount Carmel Church on Whitefriar Street. This gift was in recognition of the work undertaken by Fr John Spratt who had founded the church. A statue, carved by Irene Broe and depicting the saint in the red vestments of a martyr and holding a crocus in his hand, stands above the St Valentine altar. Here proposals of marriage are often made and people come to pray for a lifetime partner. Today the reliquary is placed before the main altar where Mass is celebrated at 11.30am and 3pm. Prayers are offered for those who are married, engaged and divorced. Engaged couples bring their wedding rings to be blessed.

Glasgow

Blessed Duns Scotus Church, part of the Franciscan Friary on Ballater Street in the Gorbals area of Glasgow, has a relic of St Valentine. A large gothic box, containing a forearm, is in an alcove in the church's modern entrance. It was given in 1868 by a French family to the Franciscans who in 1882 displayed the gift in their new Gorbals' church, St Francis in Dear Green Place. When this closed in 1993, the box was moved to nearby St Duns Scotus Church where it has been on permanent display since St Valentine's Day 1999. Morning Mass for St Cyril and St Methodius Day with hymns is followed by a procession to the shrine where prayers are said for those who are engaged, married, in difficult marriages, divorced and single.

King's Lynn

The Mart at King's Lynn is a St Valentine's Day fun fair dating from 1537 when Henry VIII granted a charter. At noon the mayor and the Bishop of Lynn led by four mace bearers arrive at the fairground in Tuesday Market Place. After a prayer and proclamation, the mayor declares the fair open and the chairman of the Showmans' Guild responds. Following a final prayer from the bishop, the VIPs ride on the dodgems. The fair remains open daily except Sunday until 27 February.

Vienna

A large chest holding St Valentine relics is in Vienna Cathedral's St Valentine's Chapel with other important relics. A Valentine Blessing Service, Valentinssegnung, started in 2006 and intended for couples, engaged couples, people in love and people looking for a partner, is held at 8pm. Around a thousand people attend and are invited to pray that they will have the courage to let each other in and be happy to create something new together. Laying on of hands and personal blessing are available at the end.

Prague

A Mass attended mainly by couples is celebrated in the presence of a relic at the Basilica of St Peter and St Paul in Vyšehrad Castle.

Roquemaure

The church of St Jean-Baptiste and St Jean-l'Evangeliste has since 1868 contained the relics of Saint Valentine brought to protect the Côtes du Rhône vineyards from phylloxera which had spread to France in 1864. Since 1988 on the Sunday before 14 February there has been a morning outdoor procession of the relics followed by Mass in church and a re-enactment of the original arrival of these relics in the afternoon.

Kiedrich, Germany

St Valentine and St Dionysius Church was raised to the status of a minor basilica by Pope Benedict XVI in 2010. The Valentine skull brought here in 1454 is in a side chapel. The gothic church dating from the fourteenth century was endowed in the nineteenth century by Augustus Pugin's friend Sir John Sutton who wished to support its unique local Gregorian choral tradition. The patronal festival is held on or near today.

Rome
Santa Maria in Cosmedin Church displays St Valentine's skull decorated with flowers, which attracts many visitors.

Bitonto, Puglia
The cathedral, dedicated to St Valentine, has a 7pm Mass followed by a love theme party.

Vico del Gargano, Puglia
Since 1618 St Valentine has been patron saint of Vico del Gargano which has a narrow street called Vicolo del Bacio (Kissing Alley). The St Valentine statue in the town's mother church is framed with oranges. After a solemn Mass at 10am the statue is carried in an outdoor procession involving several hundred people in costume. Lemon and orange blossom branches decorate the church and balconies of this hilltop town. A Valentine relic is used to bless the orange groves.

Belvedere Marittimo, Calabria
A sample of St Valentine's blood and his ashes have been at the San Daniele Convent in Belvedere Marittimo since 1710. The town's annual festival started in 2006.

San Valentino Torio
The town near Pompei exhibits the bones including Valentine's skull high above the church's altar. A street procession with a statue at 5pm is followed by Mass in the square.

Chelmno, Poland
The annual week-long festival was started in 2002 when the parish church put its Valentine relic back on display. There is a

St Valentine altar with a painting of the saint's martyrdom above. Today there is an early evening Mass. Outside a large red heart is created on the ground using candles. Shops sell special food.

Balzan, Malta
An urn in the church contains some remains of Valentine brought in 1784 from Rome and given to the parish in 1820. The saint is the church's second patron and the day is observed as a major festival.

Madrid
The skull and bones of Valentine are in a glass case below a Goya painting in San Antón in Chueca's Calle de la Hortaleza. The relics were given in the late eighteenth century by Pope Pius VI to the Royal College of San Anton and kept in the sacristy of the adjacent church. After being hidden during the Spanish Civil War they were discovered in the crypt in 1986. The St Cyril and St Methodius Mass this evening features Valentine.

St David's Day
1 March

St David

David was a fifth-century monk who lived in a monastery on the site of St David's Cathedral in Wales. He is the only patron saint in the British Isles to be a native of the country that adopted him.

He was born at St Non's Bay which is named after his mother. St David church dedications in Cornwall, Herefordshire and Brittany, in north-west France, may indicate the extent of David's travels from his Welsh homeland. His mother is buried in Dirinon Church in Brittany's Finistere.

He died at St Davids on 1 March 589. William the Conqueror made a pilgrimage to his shrine at St David's Cathedral and in about 1120 Pope Calixtus II declared David a saint and St David's Cathedral to be a place of pilgrimage.

In 1538, during the Reformation upheaval, most of the body was taken to London and burnt at Smithfield. Surviving bones were returned to the shrine when its restoration was completed in 2012.

Today at St Davids

The bishop gives the St David's Day blessing in Cross Square at noon. This evening there is Choral Eucharist with procession to the shrine and exposition of relics.

St David's Day Events

Today Welsh people, especially exiles, wear a leek or more likely a daffodil. In *Henry V* Shakespeare writes: 'Why wear you your leek today? Saint Davy's day is past.' St David is said to have suggested that Welshmen should wear a leek in their caps to distinguish them from Saxons. Leeks are presented, sometimes by the Prince of Wales or even the Queen, to Welsh troops and the youngest soldiers compete to eat raw leeks. Afterwards officers serve lunch to the junior ranks. Cawl, Welsh lamb and leek stew, is the main St David's Day dish.

The daffodil, also known as the Lent Lily, was made popular by David Lloyd George who became prime minister during World War I.

Cardiff has had a St David's Day Parade since 2004. National monuments such as the Bishop's Palace at St Davids and Caernarfon Castle are open free of charge today.

In two days' time (3 March) St Non's Day is marked at St Non's Chapel, built by the Roman Catholic Church in 1934, on the site of St David's birthplace.

St Patrick's Day

17 March

St Patrick's Day always falls in Lent and for the Irish provides a break in the Lenten abstinence. It is a public holiday in the Republic of Ireland and a Bank Holiday in Northern Ireland.

St Patrick

Patrick, patron of Ireland, was a Romano-Briton and was probably born about 390 in Wales where Irish raiders captured him to work as a herdsman. After six years he escaped and at some point around 425 trained in Britain or Europe to be a priest. In 435 he returned to Ireland as a missionary bishop, landing at Saul in County Down. In 444 he established Armagh as the primatial see. He died today in 461.

He is often depicted with snakes since he is said to be responsible for Ireland's lack of snakes by driving all of Ireland's into the sea. He is also shown holding a shamrock which, as it has three leaves, he may have used to explain the Trinity (see page 153).

Patrick's tomb, below a tenth-century cross in the grounds of Down Cathedral, is covered by a granite slab brought from the nearby Mourne Mountains in 1900 and marked simply Patric.

St Patrick's Day

St Patrick's Day is now more widely celebrated than ever having recently become part of the commercial calendar. It had been quietly observed since the ninth century and was only added to the universal calendar in 1631. It became an Irish public holiday in 1903 but within living memory Dublin was still quiet on St

Patrick's Day with all pubs closed for the day. Now Guinness invests a huge amount on advertising its stout round the world on St Patrick's Day. Since 1996 Dublin has promoted St Patrick's Day which has become a St Patrick's Festival lasting several days. In Kiltimagh County Mayo, St Patrick's Day has since 1989 been a week-long celebration of Irish culture with bands from around the world joining in a parade. Some people wear shamrock today. The oldest tradition is the annual walk up St Patrick's Mountain in Slemish, County Antrim. A bronze of St Patrick was placed in Dublin's Anglican St Patrick's Cathedral in 2001.

St Joseph of Arimathea's Day

Today is also St Joseph of Arimathea's Day. He had an important role on Good Friday when he took care of Jesus' body and provided the tomb (page 81). Joseph is also said to have brought the cup used at the Last Supper to Glastonbury. This claim is acknowledged in Bruges where, during the Precious Blood Procession on Ascension Day (see page 127), the figure of St Joseph carries a chalice.

In Church

This is a day of obligation only in Ireland although many Irish across the world attend Mass. The colour of vestments is white providing a break from the Lenten purple. In some parishes there is a blessing and distribution of shamrock at the end of Mass. In Ireland's church calendar only Holy Week and Easter can displace St Patrick's Day which even takes precedence when falling on Passion Sunday.

I bind unto myself today, known as St Patrick's Breastplate and attributed to the saint, is sung to an Irish melody. Another popular hymn is *Hail, glorious Saint Patrick*.

Today at St Patrick's Shrine

Downpatrick where St Patrick is buried holds a pilgrimage and Ireland's largest cross-community carnival parade. The Pilgrimage Walk starts at St Patrick's Church in Saul, site of the saint's arrival and a barn given to St Patrick for a church. The present small Celtic stone church with a round tower was built by the Church of Ireland in 1932 to commemorate the 1500th anniversary of Patrick's return to Ireland. Following a Eucharist at 9.15am, the walk takes just over an hour to reach Down Cathedral. Following the St Patrick's Day Pilgrimage Service, revived in 1958, a wreath is placed on St Patrick's tomb outside. Archbishop Justin Welby was a recent pilgrim. A parade of floats, dancers and people wearing fancy dress arrives in the town centre in the afternoon.

Other Celebrations

Ireland

Mass in Irish is celebrated at Dublin's Roman Catholic Pro-Cathedral and there is a Sung Eucharist at Anglican St Patrick's Cathedral. Today's Festival Parade, with lavish floats and the lord mayor's eighteenth-century coach, starts at noon at Parnell Square and takes around ninety minutes to pass down historic O'Connell Street before ending at St Patrick's Cathedral. Armagh's Anglican St Patrick's Cathedral has since 2003 celebrated the Eucharist in Irish at 10am. The main Eucharist at 12 noon is in English.

Montserrat, West Indies

In 1632 the English brought Roman Catholic Irish to the island as labourers. A rebellion by slaves on 17 March 1768 made the day special and since 1985 St Patrick's Day has been a public holiday with a festival which has grown to become a week-long celebration for African and Irish descendants. Only Ireland and Montserrat observe St Patrick's Day as a national holiday.

Nigeria

Since 1961 St Patrick has been patron of Nigeria. The consecration at Southwark Cathedral in 2017 of Nigerian-born Karowei Dorgu to be Bishop of Woolwich took place on St Patrick's Day.

London

On the Eve of St Patrick's Day there is an evening Mass and blessing of shamrock at St Patrick's Church in Soho Square, which is always attended by a huge crowd.

Kilburn is the capital's Irish quarter and the Sacred Heart Church in Quex Road, a Pugin church known as the 'Irish Cathedral', attracts large congregations for today's Masses including the main celebration at 12.15pm.

A member of the Royal Family presents shamrock to past and present members of the Irish Guards. This is usually at Wellington Barracks although it can take place outside the capital depending on deployment. The custom was begun in 1901 – a year after the Irish Guards were raised – by Queen Alexandra who sent shamrock as a gift. The Queen Mother first distributed the shamrock in 1928 and, following the death of the Princess Mary (Princess Royal) who normally carried out the engagement, did so annually from 1969. It was as a result of her long association with the Irish Guards on this day that the Queen Mother asked them to provide the bearer party at her funeral. Recently shamrock has been presented by Princess Anne, the present Princess Royal, and both the Duke and Duchess of Cambridge. In 2011, when the regiment was in Helmand, the Princess Royal's gift of shamrock was presented by Archbishop Robin Eames who was in Afghanistan.

New York

New York's St Patrick's Day parade dates from 1762 when the participants were Irish troops.

St Joseph's Day

19 March

This is another break in Lent when we recall the Virgin Mary's husband, Joseph of Nazareth.

Today is a holiday in Liechtenstein, Malta, Madrid, Spain's Basque country and the Vatican. It is Father's Day in Andorra, Bolivia, Honduras, Italy (Festa del Papà), Liechtenstein, Portugal (Dia do Pai) and Spain (Día del Padre).

St Joseph

Matthew 1 and 2; Luke 2.1-20

Little is known about the carpenter Joseph who married the Virgin Mary. He appears to have accepted the surprise and mysterious pregnancy of his fiancée with puzzlement. This gave way to calmness when the angel appears to say: 'Joseph son of David, do not be afraid to take Mary home as your wife because she has conceived, what is in her is of the Holy Spirit' (Matthew 1.20). He saved Jesus from Herod's death sentence by taking the family to Egypt.

But little is known of Joseph as he brings up his wife's son in Nazareth. Joseph may have been a builder and architect as well as a carpenter. Being much older than Mary he is thought to have died before Jesus began his public ministry.

Pope Sixtus I established today as St Joseph's solemnity in 1481. Devotion to Joseph is partly due to St Teresa of Ávila who in 1562 dedicated her new mother house in Ávila to him. Pope Gregory XV, who canonised Teresa, made his feast an obligation although this did not last. John XXIII added Joseph to the canon of the Mass (Eucharistic Prayer 1) and since 2013 he has been included in all four Roman Eucharistic prayers.

In 1870 Pius IX declared Joseph to be Patron of the Universal Church. He is the patron of carpenters and fathers and in some countries today is also Father's Day. The Inauguration Mass of Pope Francis on 19 March 2013 was a Solemnity of St Joseph. Pope Francis's coat of arms includes a symbol of Joseph.

St Joseph's Day comes just six days before the Annunciation (see page 187).

In Church

The Gloria is included in the Mass and flowers may be placed at the base of a St Joseph statue even if it is Lent. Vestments are white. The gospel can be the account of Jesus' parents searching for their lost young son and finding him in the Temple (Luke 2:41-51).

The feast is transferred if it falls on a Sunday of Lent or during Holy Week and Easter Week.

St Joseph Celebrations

Italy

A feature of the day is the cream doughnut called *zeppole* or *bignè di San Giuseppe* sold in huge numbers and with regional differences.

The biggest St Joseph's Day celebrations are in Sicily. A *San Giuseppe Tavolo*, meaning *St Joseph's Table*, which often has three tiers representing the Trinity, is erected in church or a village square and slowly laden with donations of food including bread in special shapes, cakes, frittatas, doughnuts, lemons and figs. Meatless minestrone soup is often served today with breadcrumbs sprinkled on top to resemble sawdust from Joseph's workshop.

The St Joseph doughnut, *zeppole di San Giuseppe*, is filled with ricotta cream and grated orange peel. Naples' recipe, the oldest, is dated 1837.

Being Lent there is no cheese or meat although on the coast fish may feature. A statue of St Joseph holding Baby Jesus is often included on the table. The food is blessed by the parish priest and

shared or distributed to the poor. The tradition is said to have
started in the tenth century when there was a severe drought in
Sicily and people asked St Joseph to pray for rain. When it came
they kept his day with a feast.

Valencia

Today is the climax of events known as the *Fallas* meaning
fires. Giant satirical figures displayed around the city are burnt
following a late-night flaming torch procession. The custom's
origin is the bonfire lit in honour of St Joseph by carpenters who
used their wooden pole which had held the winter lamp and
off-cuts and shavings from the floor built up during the winter
months.

The Annunciation
25 March

The Annunciation of the Blessed Virgin Mary marks the day when the Angel Gabriel appeared at the Nazareth home of Mary to announce that she would give birth to a son called Jesus. Although still a virgin she found herself to be pregnant. The angel's visit marks the conception of Jesus whose birth is celebrated on Christmas Day in nine months' time – the length of a normal pregnancy.

The Latin name for today used to be the more accurate *Conceptio Christi* meaning the *Conception of Christ*. An unofficial name was 'St Mary's Day in Lent' to distinguish it from other Marian days although the Annunciation is really a Solemnity of the Lord with a Christ-centred liturgy.

The Annunciation, the most popular religious subject in painting, has always been an important day in the calendar. Until 1582 it was the first day of the year in Europe. The British Isles continued with the old calendar as late as 1752. The tax year still observes the old calendar by beginning the year on Old Lady Day 5 April, i.e. 25 March plus the eleven days for adjustment at the time of the switch from the old Julian Calendar to the Gregorian Calendar. The 25 March date continued to be known as Lady Day and be the day when many rents fell due – as some still do. It is the day when the county high sheriffs take office.

St Bartholomew's Priory and Hospital in Smithfield was founded on the Annunciation in 1123. The first public Mass in Westminster Cathedral was celebrated today in 1903. Robert Runcie was enthroned as Archbishop of Canterbury on the Annunciation causing the Budget to be postponed for a day from the then traditional Tuesday. In 2000 Pope John Paul visited Nazareth today to celebrate Mass and the newly installed Archbishop Cormac Murphy-O'Connor of Westminster paid an ecumenical visit to Westminster Abbey.

The United Guilds service at St Paul's Cathedral takes place on the Friday nearest to 25 March. When the custom was inaugurated in 1943, as a wartime morale booster for the City, it was decided that the Annunciation was the most appropriate day.

Since 2010 today has been a public holiday in Lebanon where Christians and Muslims honour Mary. There is an Islamic-Christian prayer meeting and members of both faiths visit the shrine of Our Lady of Lebanon in Harissa. In Slovenia today is Mother's Day.

The Annunciation nearly always falls in Lent. When 25 March falls on a Sunday of Lent it is usually moved to Monday. When it falls in Holy Week or Easter Week then it is transferred to the day after Low Sunday (see page 111). It has been suggested that the crucifixion of Christ may have taken place on 25 March and very occasionally this is also Good Friday. John Donne wrote a poem about the 1608 collision. Such occasions have given rise to the saying: 'If Our Lord falls in Our Lady's lap, England will meet with a great mishap.'

Nazareth

The site of the Annunciation is now covered by the Church of the Annunciation. Some people believe that Mary was at Nazareth's well when the angel appeared and that site is St Gabriel's Greek Orthodox Church.

What Happened Today

Matthew 1.18-23 and Luke 1.26-56

Mary was in her house at the then southern end of Nazareth when the angel Gabriel appeared saying 'Rejoice, you who enjoy God's favour! The Lord is with you.' The message was that she would give birth to a baby to be called Jesus. Mary, frightened by the angel and the message, heard that her son would have 'the throne of his ancestor David' (Mary's husband Joseph was a descendant) and that 'his reign will have no end'. The angel added that her cousin Elizabeth was already six months pregnant. Mary replied: 'I am the handmaid of the Lord. Let what you have said be done to me.'

Mary's pregnancy came as a shock to her new husband who initially decided to quietly seek a divorce. (Girls were sometimes betrothed as young as 12 in advance of living with the husband.) However, his mind changed when an angel appeared to him in a dream to confirm the unprecedented situation and foretell that Jesus would 'save his people' from their sins. Mary, one day to be known as the 'God-bearer', visited Elizabeth for a long stay and afterwards she and Joseph together awaited the momentous birth.

In Church

Today can be a dramatic change in Lent with the Mass featuring a return of the Gloria, white vestments and hymns which have a reminder of Christmas. As at Christmas it is customary to kneel during the creed at the mention of the incarnation. The Christmas Season pages of Common Worship suddenly come into use today for morning and evening prayer.

The statue of Mary is surrounded by flowers even though it is Lent. If it is Passion Week (between the fifth Sunday of Lent and Palm Sunday) all this can take place with the crosses and statues veiled in purple.

Hymns might include *Sing we of the blessed mother* and *Ye who own the faith of Jesus*. *Hail Queen of Heaven* was written by historian and priest John Lingard (1771-1851) whose friend Henri Hemy provided the tune *Stella* based on a folk tune heard in the Board Inn at Stella in Blaydon-on-Tyne.

The Anglican Common Worship collect for today, a translation of the post-Communion prayer once heard in the Sarum rite on the Annunciation, acknowledges the season by looking to both Christ's birth and death on the cross.

The Hail Mary petition to the Virgin, with its first sentence taken from the angel's words, is often recited:

Hail Mary full of grace,
the Lord is with thee.
Blessed art thou amongst women
and blessed is the fruit of thy womb, Jesus.
Holy Mary, Mother of God,
pray for us sinners, now, and at the hour of our death.

Today at Nazareth

An outdoor street procession to the Church of the Annunciation takes place at 5pm on eve of the Feast of the Annunciation prior to Vespers and Benediction. The Latin patriarch of Jerusalem, accompanied by scouts and others, usually takes part. This is followed by a candlelit procession and vigil at the grotto. The main Mass today is at 10am.

Other Celebrations

Loreto, Italy
The Holy House within the church at Loreto is part of Mary's home from Nazareth. Today the statue of Our Lady and Child is dressed in a golden robe. There is a procession and Benediction at 5.45pm on the Annunciation Eve and today seven Masses including the main celebration at 6pm.

Longport-sur-Orge near Paris
Christians and Muslims hold a 'Together with Mary' prayer service this afternoon at *Notre Dame de Bonne Garde* (*Our Lady of Safekeeping*) inspired by the custom in Lebanon.

Walsingham, Norfolk
The Annunciation is an extra special day at 'England's Nazareth' in Norfolk (see page 147), where there is a noon Solemn Mass at both the Anglican and Roman Catholic shrines. Walsingham is depicted in mosaic at Nazareth's Church of the Annunciation.

Tichborne Dole
A dole at Tichborne in Hampshire this afternoon sees flour

distributed from a large wooden trough in Tichborne House porch. The Roman Catholic priest, vested in a cope, blesses the flour with holy water and censes it. This is followed by a recitation of the De Profundis for the soul of the dole founder. Then the estate manager calls out the names of those entitled to collect flour and the amount: adults qualify for a gallon and children half a gallon. The Tichborne family of Tichborne remained Roman Catholic throughout the Reformation. The ancient parish church is now Anglican but has a Roman Catholic chapel. This custom began in the thirteenth century when elderly Lady Tichborne asked her husband to give land to the villagers to produce bread. He agreed to grant only as much as she could encircle whilst holding a burning brand. Mabella Tichborne crawled round twenty-three acres which today are known as The Crawls. The distribution has been continuous except for a break, due to riotous behaviour, between 1796 and 1836. According to legend Mabella laid a curse on any successors who failed to distribute the dole. There would be a generation of seven daughters, the family name would die out and the house fall down. In 1803 Tichborne House had to be rebuilt after falling down and when Sir Henry Tichborne succeeded to the baronetcy in 1821 he produced seven daughters and no male heir. The descendants let the house on condition that the custom continues. So for about thirty minutes flour is ladled into sacks, carrier bags and plastic boxes belonging to around eighty villagers. The self-raising flour can last an entire year in some households. The distribution always takes place on 25 March even in years when the Annunciation is transferred due to Easter.

St George's Day
23 April

St George

George was martyred on 23 April in 303 in the Holy Land at Lod, the town where St Peter healed a man called Aeneas. George, almost certainly a Syrian, served in the Roman Army and was put to death under Emperor Diocletian during whose rule St Nicholas and St Lucy also died. However, George is best known for his association with the mysterious legend of killing a dragon.

The supposed and much rebuilt tomb of St George can be seen at Lod near Tel Aviv.

St George is the patron saint of England, Ethiopia, Georgia, Lithuania, Spain's Aragon and Catalonia, Moscow, Freiburg in Germany, Genoa in Italy, Istanbul, the Portuguese Army, Norwich where the Guild of St George was founded in 1389, and Scouting. He is Venice's second patron after St Mark who is celebrated in two days' time. Today has been a public holiday in Vatican City since the election of Pope Francis, Jorge (George) Bergoglio.

The Synod of Oxford, held at Osney Abbey in 1222, pronounced that St George should be the patron saint of England. Edward III founded the Order of the Garter on St George's Day 1348. Henry V invoked his name before the Battle of Agincourt and on his return to London, by way of St George the Martyr Church in Southwark, St George's Day in England was raised by the Church to greater double status. Charles II and James II both held their coronations on St George's Day. Since 1946 the monarch has filled any vacancy in the ranks of the Order of the Garter by announcing the name today.

England's oldest St George church is at Fordington, on the

edge of Dorchester in Dorset, which was built about 1100. The tympanum above the south door shows St George on horseback leading the Crusaders at the 1098 Battle of Dorylaeum, the first battle of the First Crusade.

The banner of St George, the red Greek cross of a martyr on a white background, was adopted for the uniform of English soldiers possibly in the reign of Richard I, and later became the flag of England and the White Ensign of the Royal Navy. In a seal of Lyme Regis dating from 1284 a ship is depicted bearing a flag with a cross on a plain background.

However, St George is revered not only by Christians in Europe, Ethiopia, the Middle East and India. Palestinian Muslims are often seen joining and mixing with local Christians at Lod and elsewhere at shrines dedicated to al-Khadr, as St George is known. At Beit Jala, near Bethlehem, a church marks St George's reputed birthplace.

Relics
In Rome both St John Lateran and San Giorgio in Velabro have part of the skull. St Georgio Maggiore on the Venetian Island of St Georgio also has a head claimed to be St George's. The altar of the Roman Catholic Chapel at the Royal Military Academy at Sandhurst contains a bone of St George and St George's Cathedral in Southwark holds a small relic. Yet another is found in Alcoy near Alicante in Spain.

Dragon and Roses
The dragon, often depicted with George, may represent evil or the enemy winter which ends as 23 April approaches. One suggestion is that the dragon episode is set in Libya. The rose associated with today represents the blood of the dragon supposedly slain by St George or the rose given by him to a rescued princess.

St George Associations
The Royal Society of St George was founded in 1894 with the aim of ensuring that St George's Day was 'properly celebrated'.

Queen Victoria was the patron and later Edward VII granted the Royal prefix. The Society holds a St George's Day banquet in the City of London and sends a bouquet to the Queen who in 1963 signed a Royal Charter of Incorporation.

Scouting was founded in 1907 by Robert Baden-Powell who chose St George as patron for his example of chivalry which makes war unnecessary.

In Genoa it is sometimes claimed that visiting English merchants flew the Genoese flag as their own for protection and so adopted St George for England.

The fact that today is also the birthday of William Shakespeare (1564) and J. M. W. Turner (1775) gives the day an extra resonance. In Spain the day is special for being the anniversary of the death in 1616 of both Miguel de Cervantes and Shakespeare, which has helped to encourage the spreading tradition of World Book Day.

In Church

Today, an optional commemoration, was a holy day of obligation in the universal calendar until 1778. The Church of England has restored it as a major feast.

St George's Day is sometimes transferred to another day due to Easter.

Today at Lod

The main feast day is on 16 November when large numbers of people, many Muslim, visit St George's tomb.

St George's Day customs

Dorchester

England's oldest church of St George at Fordington is open during the afternoon.

London

Southwark is the English place most associated with St George. Rebuilt St George the Martyr Church in Borough High Street, first mentioned in 1122, is the capital's oldest church with the dedication. Nearby is the galleried George Inn in the care of the National Trust. St George's Cathedral to the south was built in 1841 on St George's Fields within the ancient parish of St George the Martyr and today the cathedral displays a St George relic and celebrates with a Chapter Mass. The birthday of William Shakespeare, who knew Southwark well, is also observed at Southwark Cathedral. An Anglo-Catalan St George's Day celebration, with human towers, is held at Borough Market on the nearest Sunday.

Windsor
The Queen's Scouts hold a St George's Day Parade at Windsor Castle on the nearest Sunday afternoon and attend a service in St George's Chapel.

Modica, Sicily
After an evening Mass, a horse and dragon statue is carried around the town.

Barcelona
Sant Jordi's Day is marked by huge book sales on the pavements. The custom for the man to give the woman a rose and the woman to give the man a book continues but without any strict sexism. Book Day began in 1926 after Barcelona publisher Vicente Clavel proposed a day to honour books. There are now around two hundred book stands selling about 1.5 million books in many parts of the city, including the entire mile length of La Rambla, as well as literary and poetry events. A rose fair is held in the Palau de la Generalitat.

Alcoy, Alicante
A four-day festival includes an outdoor procession of a relic and costumed armies of 'Moorish invaders' battling with 'Christians' to take the castle amid much smoke and noise until the intervention of St George.

Taybeh, Palestine

The ruined Greek Orthodox Church at Taybeh was built in the fourth century shortly after St George was martyred. Celebrations are held in thirteen days' time according to the Julian calendar. The Christian village, almost surrounded by an Israeli settlement, has a population of just 1300 now that the majority has moved abroad.

St Mark's Day
25 April

St Mark

Mark 14.51; Acts 12.12 and 25; 15.39; Col 4.10; 1 Peter 5.13

St Mark the Evangelist, also called John Mark, is the author of St Mark's Gospel which he wrote in Rome. He had lived in Jerusalem and he may have been describing himself when he wrote of the young man who escaped capture by running away naked when Christ was arrested in the Garden of Gethsemane (see page 71). His mother's house was a meeting place for the Apostles and St Peter went there when freed from prison. Mark was part of St Paul's first missionary journey, preached in Cyprus with St Barnabas, and was with St Paul in Rome.

Mark, who founded the Church in Egypt, was probably martyred. His body was brought by merchants from Alexandria in Egypt in 829 to Venice where his tomb is now visible within the high altar at St Mark's Basilica.

Alexandria's Coptic cathedral holds relics including some returned by Venice in 1968.

Today in Venice

The main Mass in St Mark's is celebrated by the patriarch with a procession and trumpets at 10am. As recorded by the artist Bellini in 1496 there used to be an outdoor procession round St Mark's Square with the relics.

The day is also observed with a gondoliers' regatta and by men giving a red rose to wives, girlfriends and mothers.

May Day
1 May

Today is both May Day and the Feast of St Joseph the Worker as well as the start of the month of Mary. It was universally St Philip and St James Day although this was overshadowed even before the Reformation by May Day revels. The May Day carol *The winter's sleep was long and deep* by Percy Dearmer mentions 'two saints of God'.

St Joseph the Worker

See St Joseph (page 184).

Month of Mary

The origin of May as Mary's month can be found in about 1826 when a book of May devotions was written by Italian Jesuit Anniblae Dionisis. Later in the century, Father Latomia introduced the idea to the Roman Jesuit College and the custom soon spread to other colleges. This tradition of Mary's month with a May procession and crowning the statue of Mary was brought to England in 1840 by Italian father of charity Aloysius Gentili. Since 1979 the climax has been The Visitation (see page 203) on 31 May.

The May Queen tradition has been kept alive in many schools thanks to Whitelands College (University of Surrey) where student teachers experience May Queen festivities started in 1881 by John Ruskin.

Workers' Day

In 1833 mill owner Robert Owen said that 1 May should be a festival of labour. But it was six deaths in Chicago on May

Day 1886 during a workers' demonstration for an eight-hour day that led to a call three years later in Paris by the International Workingmen's Association for the day to be declared a holiday. The idea of May Day as a workers' day, with pride in skills and class, spread rapidly.

It was to give this movement a Christian dimension that in 1955 Pope Pius XII designated May Day as the Feast of St Joseph the Worker, Mary's working husband. The May Day gathering of workers and their families in St Peter's Square addressed by the Pope easily overshadowed Rome's communist rallies.

St Philip and St James Day

St Joseph the Worker Day displaced the saints' day which moved to 3 May in the Roman calendar. Philip, an Apostle, is patron of Luxembourg. James, another Apostle, is known as St James the Less.

Maypole

The origin of the maypole which features in May Day celebrations is unknown but the version with ribbons for dancers to hold may only date from the eighteenth century. St Andrew Undershaft Church in the City of London takes its name from the prominent maypole that was situated outside until 1547.

May Day Events

Ansty, Wiltshire

The first maypole was erected in the sixteenth century and tonight there is a May Queen crowning and maypole dancing.

Charlton-on-Otmoor, Oxfordshire

Children carrying a garland and individual flower crosses arrive this morning outside the church where the rector blesses the garland with holy water. The cross on the church rood screen is already covered with foliage and the garland, representing the missing figure of Our Lady, is added. After the singing of two May hymns there is dancing outside. The bringing of floral crosses to church, rather than taking them door to door and singing, dates from 1963 but the garland custom has been maintained almost unbroken since the Reformation.

King's Lynn, Norfolk

A May Garland Procession starts at noon outside St Margaret's Church in Saturday Market Place. Over two hours a large garland of flowers, greenery and beads surrounding a doll is carried on the end of a pole accompanied by the blowing of ox horns. The tradition was revived in 1983 by the King's Morris who also blow a horn at dawn.

London

From the 1790s chimney sweeps have dressed up as the green man, Jack-in-the-Green, today. Completely covered in greenery, the figure walked the streets with fellow sweeps who had streamers tied to their clothes. A Jack-in-the-Green still appears in Deptford.

Minehead, Somerset

At 6am a man elaborately dressed as the Hobby Horse, or 'Obby 'Oss, proceeds from the Quay and around town all day and then on to Yarn Market, Dunster Castle and Dunster Village in the evening. It proceeds through Minehead over the next two evenings with attendants known as Gullivers. Everywhere it goes the Horse Dance tune is played on accordion and drums. The origin is uncertain but it is ancient.

Oxford

At 6am twenty-nine choristers sing from the top of Magdalen College's 144 foot Great Tower. It is not known why the custom developed or how old it is but the tower was completed in 1505 and by 1674 tower top singing at 4am was described as 'an ancient custom'. Bad weather early in the seventeenth century forced the singing to be put back an hour and that year the choristers sang the *Hymnus Eucharisticus* which had been written and composed at the college and was well-known to them. It has featured ever since. In the early nineteenth century town boys regularly came to bang tins and blow penny whistles which led to the choirboys above retaliating in 1840 with rotten eggs. The bursar, Dr J. R. Bloxham, an Anglo-Catholic known as 'the father of all ritualists', insisted on keeping the May Day tradition. Now, depending on the weather, at least 4000 people, many students, gather below. But Magdalen Bridge has been closed annually since 1998 to dissuade people from jumping into the shallow River Cherwell. Afterwards the tower bells ring out and a Sung Eucharist for St Philip and St James Day follows in the chapel at 9.15am.

Oundle, Northamptonshire
At Oundle School today (or Bank Holiday Monday) sixteenth-century madrigals, including *Now is the month of Maying* by Thomas Morley, are sung from the Cloisters Tower at 7.15am. The twenty-minute custom began in 2002.

Padstow, Cornwall
The crowded town is decorated with the greenery and flowers along with a maypole for a tradition which may go back to the fourteenth century. The 'Obby 'Oss, a disguised human dressed in a circular wooden frame draped with black material, spends the day until late at night touring the narrow streets accompanied by music and dancers. A second one is called the Blue Ribbon Oss. Much heard is the May Day song: 'Unite and unite let us all unite/For summer is a come unto day/And whither we are going we will all unite/In the merry morning of May.'

Sturminster Marshall, Dorset
The maypole dancing, now on May Day Monday Bank Holiday morning, began in 1101.

Germany
Tall maypoles, without ribbons but sometimes painted, are found in Bavaria.

St Matthias Day
14 May

Until 1968 St Matthias Day was on 24 February. The present date is more appropriate as it was after the Ascension but before Pentecost that Matthias was chosen to replace Judas as an Apostle (see page 65). Today often falls between the Ascension and Pentecost.

St Matthias
Acts 1.15-26

Matthias and Joseph Barsabbas Justus, who had known Jesus since his baptism, were chosen as candidates to fill the vacancy. Matthias won the selection held among the hundred and twenty followers who drew lots although soon, on choosing deacons including Stephen, the method was to be election.

Matthias's tomb is at St Matthias' Abbey in Trier, Germany.

The Visitation
31 May

Today recalls the arrival of Mary at her cousin Elizabeth's house. The special day, originating in Constantinople and universal from 1389, was observed on 2 July until 1969.

Mary's visit could have occurred within a few days of the Annunciation (see page 186). Elizabeth, pregnant with John the Baptist, lived a hundred and thirty-five miles away at the village of Ein Kerem near Jerusalem.

Visitation Site at Ein Kerem

The Church of the Nativity of St John the Baptist is on a site where Elizabeth is reputed to have lived and where Mary and Elizabeth met. The Spring of the Virgin is where Mary and Elizabeth are said to have drawn water. Another church, The Visitation, has the words of the Magnificat in forty-five languages on its courtyard walls. Upstairs is a stone behind which baby John was allegedly hidden from King Herod's soldiers.

What Happened Today

Luke 1.39-56

As Mary entered the house, Elizabeth felt her own baby move inside her. This was John the Baptist acknowledging Jesus. Elizabeth called out: 'Of all women you are the most blessed, and blessed is the fruit of your womb.' This is the origin of the second sentence of the Hail Mary prayer (see page 190).

Mary's response was to praise God with words anticipating the teaching of her son Jesus. It is a triumphal and revolutionary blueprint song foretelling the reversal of order and a topsy-turvy future. It is also a preview not only of the Epiphany, when Jesus is visited by kings rather than being taken to them, but also of the Sermon on the Mount preached thirty years later. The song, known as the Magnificat, reflects the words of Hannah after the birth of her child as recorded in the Old Testament (1 Samuel 2).

Mary stayed with Elizabeth for three months and so was probably present at the birth of John the Baptist which is celebrated on St John's Day, 24 June.

The Magnificat begins with the familiar words *My soul doth magnify the Lord* (Book of Common Prayer) heard at evening prayer.

At The Visitation Site Today

There is a Mass this morning in the Church of The Visitation which stands on the supposed spot at Ein Kerem where Mary and Elizabeth met and above a spring associated with them.

BIBLIOGRAPHY

Ackroyd, Peter, *Shakespeare: The Biography*, Chatto and Windus, 2005.

Allison, Ronald and Riddell, Sarah, *The Royal Encyclopedia*, Macmillian, 1991.

Arnold-Forster, Frances, *Studies in Church Dedications*, Skeffington, 1899.

Barron, Caroline and Saul, Nigel, *England and The Low Countries in the Late Middle Ages*, Sutton, 1995.

Baxter, Philip, *Sarum Use, Sarum Script*, 1994.

Beeson, Trevor, *Window on Westminster*, SCM Press, 1998.

Blair, John, *The Church in Anglo-Saxon Society*, Oxford, 2005.

Bogle, Joanna, *A Book of Feasts and Seasons*, Gracewing, 1988.

Bowker, John, *The Complete Bible Handbook*, Dorling Kindersley, 1998.

Bradley, Ian, *Pilgrimage: A Spiritual and Cultural Journey*, Lion, 2009.

Bradley, Ian, *The Penguin Book of Hymns*, Penguin, 1990.

Bradshaw, Paul F. and Johnson, Maxwell E., *The Origins of Feasts, Fasts and Seasons in Early Christianity*, SPCK, 2011.

Brown, David, *Tradition and Imagination*, Oxford, 1999.

Carey, George, *The Bible for Everyday Life*, Lion, 2000.

Chandler, Andrew and Hein, David, *Archbishop Fisher 1945-1961: Church, State and World*, Ashgate, 2012.

Clarke, John, *Church Services for the Farming Year*, National Agricultural Centre, 1988.

Cooper, Quentin and Sullivan, Paul, Maypoles, *Martyrs and Mayhem*, Bloomsbury, 1994.

Cottiaux, Jean, *Sainte Julienne de Cornillon*, Carmel de Cornillon, 1991.

Davidson, Linda Kay and Gititz, David M., *Pilgrimage*, ABC-CLIO, 2002.

Drake-Carnell, F.J., *Old English Customs and Ceremonies*, Batsford, 1938.

Dudley, Martin, *Ashes to Glory*, SPCK, 1999.

Duffy, Eamon, *The Stripping of the Altars*, Yale, 1992.

Farmer, David Hugh, *Oxford Dictionary of Saints*, OUP, 1987

Farncombe, Anne, *The Easter Book*, National Christian Education Council, 1984.

Feasey, Henry John, *Ancient English Holy Week Ceremonial*, Thomas Baker, 1897.

Fells, Maurice, *The Bristol Year: Ancient and Modern City Traditions*, Broadcast, 2003.

Fenton, J. C., *The Gospel According to John*, Oxford, 1970.

Fenton, J. C., *St Matthew*, Pelican, 1963.

Ferguson, James, *The Emmerdale Book of Country Lore*, Hamlyn, 1988.

Field, John, *Place-Names of Greater London*, Batsford, 1980.

Fox, Michael and Peter, *A Saddleworth Whitsuntide*, St Chad's Church Saddleworth, 1990.

Galbiati, Enrico, *The Gospel of Jesus*, Vicenza, Instituto S. Gaetiano, 1970.

Gaeta, Francis X, *Come – Celebrate Jesus!*, Resurrection Press New York, 1997.

Gascoigne, Margaret, *Discovering English Customs and Traditions*, Shire, 1969.

Goddard, Philip J., *Festa Paschalia*, Gracewing 2012.

Griffiths, Alan, *Celebrating the Christian Year: Vol II*, Canterbury Press, 2005.

Grigson, Jane, Vegetable Book, Penguin, 1978.

Guarita, Carlos, *Theatre of the Seasons*, Lisboa Camara Municipal, 1999.

Haffner, Paul, *The Mystery of Mary*, Gracewing, 2004.

Harrison, Frederick, *Medieval Man and His Notions*, John Murray, 1947.

Harrowven, Jean, *Origins of Festivals and Feasts*, Pryor, 1980.

Heales, A., *Easter Sepulchres*, Archaeologia, 1869.

Herbert, William, *History of the Worshipful Company of Skinners of London*, Lightning Source, 2012

Hole, Christina, *A Dictionary of British Folk Customs*, Paladin, 1987.

Hole, Christina, *Easter and Its Customs*, Richard Bell, 1961.

Hole, Christina, *English Traditional Customs*, Batsford, 1975.

Humphreys, Colin J., *The Mystery of the Last Supper*, Cambridge, 2011.

Jones C.P.A, *A Manual for Holy Week*, SPCK, 1967.

Knightly, Charles, *The Customs and Ceremonies of Britain*, Thames and Hudson, 1986.

Lambarde, William, *Alphabetical Description of Chief Places in England and Wales*, 1730.
le Vay, Benedict, *Eccentric Britain*, Bradt, 2000.
Leeming, Bernard, *The Churches and The Church*, DLT, 1963.
Livingstone, E.A., *Concise Dictionary of the Christian Church*, Oxford, 1977.
Long, George, *The Folklore Calendar*, Senate, 1930.
Longford, Lord, *The Life of Jesus Christ*, Sidgwick and Jackson, 1974.

McDonald, James, *Alnwick Castle: The Home of the Duke and Duchess of Northumberland*, Frances Lincoln, 2012.
Marini, Piero, *A Challenging Reform: Realizing the Vision of the Liturgical Renewal, 1963-1975*, Liturgical Press, 2008.
Marshall, Rob, *The Transfiguration of Jesus*, DLT, 1994.
Martin, Elizabeth, *Sandwich Almshouses 1190-1975*, Sandwich Local History Society, 1974.
McArthur, A. Allan, *The Evolution of the Christian Year*, SCM, 1953.
Metford, J. C. J., *The Christian Year*, Thames and Hudson, 1991.
Morison, John and Daisley, Peter, *Hare Pie Scrambling and Bottle Kicking*, Hallaton Museum Press, 2000.
Mulder-Bakker, Anneke B., *Living Saints of the Thirteenth Century*, Brepols, 2011.
Musto, Walter, *The War and Uncle Walter*, Bantam, 2004.

O'Donovan, Patrick, *A Journalist's Odyssey*, Esmonde Publishing, 1985.
Oldfield, Paul, *Sanctity and Pilgrimage in Medieval Southern Italy, 1000-1200*, Cambridge 2014.
O'Loughlin, Thomas, *Liturgical Resources for Lent and Eastertide*, Columbia, 2004.

Packenham, Thomas, *Meeting with Remarkable Trees*, Weidenfeld, 1996.
Palmer, Geoffrey and Lloyd, Noel, *A Year of Festivals*, Warne, 1972.
Palmer, Roy, *Britain's Living Folklore*, David and Charles, 1991.
Perham, Michael, *Celebrate the Christian Story*, SPCK, 1997.
Perham, Michael, *Liturgy Pastoral and Parochial*, SPCK, 1996.

Raby, Ivan, *The Silver Ball*, Raby, 1991.

Ratcliffe, E. E., *The Royal Maundy*, The Royal Maundy Office, 1948.

Ratzinger, Joseph (Benedict XVI), *Jesus of Nazareth: Holy Week*, Catholic Truth Society, 2011.

Reid, Alcuin, *The Organic Development of the Liturgy*, Saint Michael's Abbey Press, 2004.

Rowe, Doc, *May Day: The Coming of Spring*, English Heritage, 2006.

Rubin, Miri, *Corpus Christi*, Cambridge, 1991.

Ryan, Vincent, *Lent and Holy Week*,Veritas, 1976.

Simpson, Jaqueline and Round, Steve, *A Dictionary of English Folklore*, Oxford, 2000.

Smith, C. Penswick, *The Revival of Mothering Sunday*, The Mothering Sunday Movement, 1932.

Smyth, Charles, *Good Friday at St Margaret's*, Mowbray, 1957.

Snell, F. J., *The Customs of Old England*, Methuen, 1911.

Sox, David, *Relics and Shrines*, Allen and Unwin, 1985.

Sykes, Homer, *Once a Year*, Gordon Fraser, 1977.

Symonds, Richard, *Diary of the Marches of the Royal Army*, Cambridge, 1998.

Tasker, R. V. G., *St Matthew*, Tyndale, 1961.

Tavinor, Michael, *Shrines of the Saints in England and Wales*, Canterbury, 2016.

Urlin, Ethel L., *Festivals, Holy Days and Saints' Days: A Study in Origins and Survivals in Church Ceremonies and Secular Customs*, Simpkin, Marshall, Hamilton, Kent, 1915.

Vipont, Elfrida, *Some Christian Festivals*, Michael Joseph, 1963.

Walsh, Michael, *The Universe Book of Saints*, Geoffrey Chapman, 1994.

Wareham, Norman and Gill, Jill, *Every Pilgrim's Guide to the Holy Land*, Canterbury, 1998.

Weinreb, Ben and Hibbert, Christopher, *Encyclopaedia of London*, Macmillan, 1983.

Whistler, Laurence, *The English Festivals*, Heinemann, 1947.

Wilson, Jan, *Feasting for Festivals*, Sandy Lane Books, 1990.

Wright, Peter, *The Story of the Royal Maundy*, Pitkin, 1990.